Y0-BTA-721

Medieval Catalan Literature: Prose and Drama

Twayne's World Authors Series
Spanish Literature

Donald W. Bleznick, Editor
University of Cincinnati

Janet Pérez, Editor
Texas Tech University

TWAS 802

Frontispiece of the Regiment de la cosa pública by Francesc Eiximenis. Incunabulum 276 of the Biblioteca Universitaria de Valencia.

Medieval Catalan Literature: Prose and Drama

by David J. Viera

Tennessee Technological University

Twayne Publishers
A Division of G. K. Hall & Co. • Boston

Medieval Catalan Literature: Prose and Drama

David J. Viera

Copyright 1988 by G.K. Hall & Co.
All rights reserved.
Published by Twayne Publishers
A Division of G.K. Hall & Co.
70 Lincoln Street
Boston, Massachusetts 02111

Copyediting supervised by Barbara Sutton
Book production by Gabrielle B. McDonald
Book design by Barbara Anderson

Typeset in 11 pt. Garamond
by Williams Press, Inc., Albany, New York

Printed on permanent/durable acid-free paper
and bound in the United States of America

Library of Congress Cataloging in Publication Data

Viera, David J.
    Medieval Catalan literature: prose and drama / David J. Viera.

    p.   cm.—(Twayne's world authors series ; TWAS 802. Spanish literature)
    Bibliography: p. 105
    Includes index.
    ISBN 0-8057-8233-8 (alk. paper)
    1. Catalan literature—To 1500—History and criticism.   I. Title.
II. Series: Twayne's world authors series ; TWAS 802.   III. Series:
Twayne's world authors series. Spanish literature.
PC3909.V54   1988
849'.98108'09—dc19   87-33119
                                                                   CIP

To Carroll

Contents

About the Author

David J. Viera is professor of Spanish at Tennessee Technological University. He received his M.A. and Ph.D. degrees from Catholic University of America and has taught at the State University of New York College at Geneseo. He has published over fifty articles on Catalan, Spanish, and Portuguese literature and is the author of two books on Francesc Eiximenis: *Bibliografia anotada de la vida i obra de Francesc Eiximenis* (1981) and *La dona en Francesc Eiximenis* (1987).

Preface

As Catalan-Aragonese military conquests spread east and south, a literature in Catalan developed in the newly acquired territories. Ramon Llull found his inspiration in his native Mallorca; Francesc Eiximenis produced his mature works in his adopted city, Valencia; Vincent Ferrer delivered vernacular sermons in his native Valencia; Ramon Muntaner immortalized the Catalan-Aragonese conquests in Italy and Greece by his eyewitness accounts of heroic deeds. To record their thoughts, religious beliefs, and histories, these authors wrote in prose, the major literary form in which Catalan literature appeared.

I begin by describing the early manifestations of Catalan prose and continue to the first decades of the fifteenth century. In subsequent chapters I take up one of the most prolific authors of the late Middle Ages, Ramon Llull, and other leading figures of Catalan religious prose literature—Arnau de Vilanova, Francesc Eiximenis, and Vincent Ferrer—whom I discuss chronologically. In another section I describe, analyze, and compare the major chronicles of four authors: James I, Bernat Desclot, Ramon Muntaner, and Peter III. Finally, I end with a chapter on leading works of medieval Catalan theater, both religious and secular, including fifteenth-century revisions of lost thirteenth- and fourteenth-century dramatic works.

My purpose is to acquaint the medievalist, generalist, and Hispanist with the medieval prose and drama written in Catalan. Preceding the analysis of his works, I have included information on the life of each author, his literary importance during his time, and his influence on future generations. I have relied on extant translations of several works by Llull and the four major chronicles, citing the source in a footnote or in parentheses following the citation. All other translations are mine. To provide for future study, a selected bibliography and an index close the volume.

Since the counts of Barcelona became kings of Aragon after 1137 and of Valencia in 1238, their names and the numerals following their names vary. For example, Pedro IV of Aragon became Pere III of Catalonia and Pere II of Valencia, and Alfonso II of Aragon became Alfons I of Catalonia. For simplicity, I have given English names and Catalan rather than the Aragonese or Valencian numerals to Catalan kings (for example, Peter III, Alphonse I of Catalonia). Also, I use Catalan names for critics who used a Spanish variant. For example, M. Milà i Fontanals replaces the Spanish equivalent M. Milá y Fontanals, and Jordi Rubió i Balaguer replaces Jorge Rubió y Balaguer. However, the footnotes and bibliography retain the forms of the author's name as it appears in the bibliographic reference.

To my knowledge this is the first survey in English of medieval Catalan literature; however, this volume focuses only on prose and drama of belletristic value and does not consider translations, letters, legal compilations, and maritime regulations. Also, I have omitted poetry because the troubadours from Catalan-speaking areas wrote in Provençal.

I end the prose section with Vincent Ferrer's death in 1419. As a continuation to the present volume, Patricia J. Boehne will publish *The Renaissance Novel*, which includes such authors as Anselm Turmeda, Bernat Metge, Jaume Roig, and others who represent a transition from medieval to Renaissance Catalan literature.

I wish to express my gratitude to several people who contributed to this study. Professors Curt J. Wittlin, Josep Miquel Sobré, and John Dagenais read and offered suggestions on selected chapters. Professor William Fisk and Mrs. Peggy Jolly helped with proofreading the manuscript. Tennessee Technological University funded the typing of my manuscript. Lastly, a special thanks to my wife, Carroll Viera, to whom this book is dedicated, for her patience, and for reading and advice on the manuscript.

David J. Viera

Tennessee Technological University

Chronology

1327 Alphonse III succeeds James II.

1336 Peter III succeeds Alphonse III.

1343 The Balearic Islands are annexed by Catalonia.

1346 Beginning of the Hundred Years War.

1348–1351 Plague of the Black Death in Catalonia.

1350 Birth of Vincent Ferrer.

1354 Reconquest of Sardinia.

1378 Beginning of the Great Western Schism.

1379 Eiximenis begins the *Primer del Crestià* (First book of the Christian).

1385 *Crònica de Pere III* (*Chronicle* of Peter III).

1387 John I replaces Peter III.

1391 Death and destruction in the Jewish quarters takes place throughout Iberia.

1409 Death of Eiximenis. Council of Pisa.

1410–1412 Compromise of Caspe.

1418 Great Western Schism ends.

1419 Death of Vincent Ferrer.

Chapter One
Origin and First Manifestations of Catalan Literature

In the tenth and eleventh centuries Catalans enjoyed a brief respite from their reconquest of the original Catalonia or *Marca Hispanica,* a Carolingian buffer state between France and Moorish-dominated Spain. During this time they regrouped, codified their laws and history, and created their own art and music. Between 1018 and 1068 they formed Catalan peace assemblies, often presided over by Oliba (ca. 971–1046), abbot of Cuxa and Ripoll (1008–46) and bishop of Vic (1017–46), who founded monasteries such as Montserrat and rebuilt monasteries and churches in the diocese of Vic. During his time the monastic library at Ripoll grew with valuable manuscripts, and Catalan historiography began at Ripoll and Cuxa (see chapter 4). In addition, under Count Ramon Berenguer I (1035–76) Catalans promulgated the *usatges* (1068), judicial proceedings that formed the basis of their constitutional government.

Churches, monasteries, and the courts of Catalan counts became centers of Catalan culture. In art, Catalonia produced several Romanesque frescos that date from the eleventh to the thirteenth century. Religious sculpture was also evident at monasteries of Roussillon and at Sant Pere de Roda (Crues) in the eleventh century. A popular culture developed simultaneously and interdependently of monastic and courtly circles and gradually came to define, to a large extent, the character of Catalan art, music, and literature. Unfortunately, Catalan poetry, which emanated from a traditional popular vein, has been lost.

In 1901 the manuscript of what may be the oldest known work of Catalonia was discovered: *Cançó de Santa Fe* (Song of St. Fides) (ca. 1030–70). According to Ernest Hoepffner, this work was written in a language spoken in an area north of the eastern Pyrenees, which Prosper Alfaric specified as the Abbey of Cuxa (Prades),[1] and Martí Jampy as the monastery of Sant Martí de Canigó, insisting that it was written in the language of Roussillon.[2] Today, however, scholars are in disagreement about the language in which the poem was written: Catalan or Provençal.[3] The text, 593 lines of octosyllabic verse, may be divided into three sections: a brief introduction (stanzas 1–3); the martydom of the twelve-year-old girl Fides of Agen by the pagan Dacian (4–43); and an invective against the Roman rulers, two of whom were Dacian's superiors (44–55).

As a literary work this poem lacks unity, clarity, and order. Despite unoriginal images and undeveloped characters, the anonymous poet carefully selected from accounts of Fides's life and left his imprint through the dramatic scenes (death of Diocletian), animated dialogues, and conviction he added to the work. Despite digressions and enumerations, the last part is more original and personal because the author seems less dependent on sources.

The fragment of *Forum judicum* (Laws of the judges) in Catalan, translated probably in the twelfth century, is the oldest prose text in the Catalan language.[4] A translation of Visigothic law with interpolated glosses, this short piece is important for its clear Catalan vocabulary and idiomatic structures.

Sermons were among the first literary manifestations of Romance languages because lay Christians in the Middle Ages did not know Latin. The Council of Rheims (813) approved of sermons preached in Romance languages so that laypersons would receive moral lessons. The discovery of an incomplete set of sermons at the parish of Organyà (Lérida), appropriately titled *Homilies d'Organyà* (Homilies of Organya), confirms vernacular preaching.[5] Sometimes considered the "Standard of reference for pre-literary Catalan,"[6] *Homilies d'Organyà* consist of gospel notes and commentaries and biblical passages. This collection of eight sermons, six of which are incomplete, dates from the end of the twelfth to the early thirteenth century. The invocatory form *Seinors* (Sires) and the function of Organyà as a collegiate church indicate that these sermons were preached to Augustinian Canons Regular on different Sundays in the Church calendar.

According to Maurice Molho, homilies 2, 3, 5, and 6 follow a traditional medieval sermonic technique and are superior to sermons 1 and 4, both of which incorporate the modern art of preaching.[7] These sermons, for the most part, consist of memoranda to aid in preaching and are often fragmentary. Also, they are written in a direct, plain language and simple, natural style and have some literary interest. Despite their structural similarity to twelfth-century Provençal sermons,[8] the influence of the Provençal language is insignificant. Although religious verse was transmitted orally, some poems survive, such as "Aujats senyors qui credets Déu lo Paire" (Listen, sirs, who believe in God the father), an anonymous thirteenth-century *plantus Mariae* (lament of Mary) based on French and Provençal models.[9] Also, the thirteenth-century *virolais* (based on the French *virelai*) testify that poems sung and accompanied by dance existed in Catalan-speaking areas.[10] Examples of Catalan songs chanted by pilgrims and *goigs,* poems praising Mary and other saints, have also been located.

Chapter Two

Ramon Llull

Biography

Biographers have reconstructed Ramon Llull's life from legal documents, his works, and *Vita coetanea* (Contemporary life, 1311).[1] Llull was born of noble lineage in the city of Mallorca between 1232 and 1233.[2] In his youth he became known in the court of James I and befriended the king's son James II of Mallorca (1276–1311), whom he later served as seneschal.

After his thirtieth year, Llull underwent a spiritual crisis, brought about by five visions of Christ crucified.[3] Interpreting these visions as a divine message, he dedicated himself to three projects for Christ: converting infidels, writing to combat non-Catholic beliefs, and promoting monasteries in which to teach missionaries Oriental languages.

After providing for his family, Llull began a pilgrimage to Santiago de Compostela, Rocamadour, and other shrines. Realizing he needed a background in the liberal arts and theology, he planned to attend the University of Paris. But since Ramon de Penyafort convinced him to study in Mallorca, he received his academic training either at the Cistercian monastery of La Real or at Mallorcan libraries. In Mallorca he learned Arabic from a Moorish slave and read the works of Algazel and other Arab authorities.

Following nine years of study, Llull spent twenty days in contemplation on Mount Randa, where he conceived "through divine illumination" the works known as his "Art." From Randa he returned to La Real to compose his *Ars compendiosa inveniendi* (Brief Art of finding truth, ca. 1274).[4]

Llull spent 1275 to 1279 in two locations: Montpellier and Miramar (Mallorca). At Miramar, he requested financial aid from James of Mallorca to establish a college there. Pope John XXI approved the project, which James funded, and in 1276 thirteen Franciscans began studying theology, liberal arts, Oriental languages, Islamic culture and beliefs, and Llull's Art.

4

Llull returned to Rome in 1287 to interest Pope Honorius IV in his projects and to inform the pontiff of his success; however, the pope's death and the indifference of the Roman curia to his projects forced him to leave for Paris to lecture on his Art. At the Sorbonne he realized his Art was too complex. Therefore, he reduced the combinations of figures in his *Art inventiva veritatis* (Art of finding truth) from sixteen to four.[5]

Llull advocated peaceful conversion of non-Catholics. However, when Pope Nicholas IV rejected his missionary and military proposals (1290), he began supporting a military crusade. Between 1291 and 1292 Llull underwent a crisis in Genoa. As he was about to sail to Barbary, doubts and fears overtook him. *Vita coetanea* relates: "There came to him on several occasions a kind of fixed idea that if he traveled to the land of Saracens they would slaughter him the moment he arrived, or at the very least would throw him into prison forever" (*SW*, 1:30).

Having scandalized the Genovese by withdrawing from his sacred mission, Llull experienced another spiritual crisis and a serious illness, which delayed his trip. But around 1293 he arrived in Tunis, where he debated religious matters with learned Moors. There, suspected of wanting to destroy the Islamic religion, he was reported to the caliph and imprisoned and then insulted, beaten, and expelled.

In April 1294 Llull settled in Naples to preach and write works including his *Flors d'amors e flors d'intel.ligència* (Flowers of love and flowers of intelligence). There he petitioned Pope Celestine V to found colleges, conquer the Holy Land, and unify military orders. Celestine's papal resignation and the indifference of his successor, Boniface VIII, convinced Llull to leave Naples and to seek help from James II of Mallorca, who recommended him to his nephew Philip IV of France. Llull traveled to Paris, where he gained several disciples and wrote *Arbre de filosofia d'amor (The Tree of Love)*.[6]

After hearing that the khan of Tartary had conquered Syria (ca. 1301), Llull set out for the Holy Land. However, realizing in Cyprus that a Tartar victory had been falsely reported, he remained on this island but was not allowed to proselytize heretics. After another unsuccessful attempt to obtain papal approval to conquer the Holy Land, Llull sailed to Bougie to proselytize Muslims. Again he was rescued from an enraged crowd, imprisoned, and expelled. His expulsion canceled his religious debate with learned Muslims, which he had written in Arabic. Later he rewrote in Pisa (1308) a Latin version, *Disputatio Raymundi christiani et Hamar sarraceni* (Disputation of Ramon the

Christian and Hamar the Saracen), because the Arabic original had been lost in a shipwreck.

The Council of Vienne (October 1311) renewed Llull's hopes for converting non-Catholics. To prepare for the assembly, Llull composed, among other works, *Petitio in concilio generali* (Petition to the general council) and *Lo concili* (The council), which contained proposals, most of which were rejected. Now in his eighties, Llull returned to Mallorca, continued writing, and made his will. In May 1313, he traveled to the Sicilian court of Frederick III,[7] but since the Sicilian court did not satisfy his missionary zeal, he sailed for Tunis, where he arrived in 1315. The peaceful accord between Sancho of Mallorca—James II of Mallorca died in 1311—and the king of Tunis, and recommendations to the latter from James II of Aragon, allowed Llull to preach, discuss Christian beliefs with Saracens, and continue writing. Llull died between December 1315 and March 1316, probably on a return to Mallorca, and was buried in Palma de Mallorca.

General Observations on His Works and Art

Llull's work varies in length, subject matter, and medium of expression. He wrote speculative, scientific, didactic, social, and mystical works,[8] and composed prose in Arabic, Catalan, and Latin. Although he spoke and wrote in Latin and knew its grammar,[9] he often relied on his followers to translate his works into Latin. Llull has been called the creator of Catalan literary prose, a claim that critics challenged after comparing his language and syntax to that of the prose of James I, Desclot, and Arnau de Vilanova. Although he advanced erudite Catalan prose, Llull's major innovation consisted of providing the layperson knowledge written in the vernacular of fields such as philosophy, theology, astronomy, and rhetoric (*OE*, 2:130).[10]

Because Llull wrote to glorify God and to make God's teaching and love known, creating works of literary merit was of secondary concern. However, he was conscious of style and semantics, believing that the beauty of each word is contained in its meaning. Aware of the inadequacy of language, he created neologisms (*OE*, 2:1332–58) and expressed complex ideas in metaphors, proverbs, and *exempla*. Also he developed opinions on style in *Rhetorica nova* (New rhetoric), *Llibre de contemplació en Déu*, (Book of contemplation) and *Doctrina pueril* (Instruction for boys), among other works, and provided manuals for preaching to infidels that stress innovative methods and ideas rather than phonetic and stylistic devices.[11]

In *Ars compendiosa inveniendi,* Llull reduced all knowledge to God's dignities or divine attributes, which become principles to discover truth. He then related the dignities, generally equivalent to the Platonic Ideas, to the techniques of his *ars combinatoria,* a combinatory method that, when applied to theological beliefs, would convince infidels of the Catholic faith. Llull explained his Art in a large section of his works. For example, he attempted to simplify and apply his Art in *Ars demonstrativa* (Demonstrative Art), *Taula general* (General table), and *Ars inventiva* (Inventive Art). *Art generalis ultima* (Last general Art, 1305–8) represents the finished product of a thirty-year revision. In addition, nine works deal with the usefulness of the Art in astronomy, geometry, physics, and medicine.[12]

Catalan Works

After studying nine years at Mallorca, Llull wrote *Llibre de contemplació* (ca. 1273–74) in Arabic, revised it in Catalan, and divided it into three volumes in honor of the Trinity. The three volumes contain five books for Christ's wounds, forty "distinctions" (sections) for Christ's days in the desert, 365 chapters for the days of the year, and a final chapter that explains how to use the work, summarizes his aims, and offers critical comments.[13]

Judging from its length, thoroughness, and subtlety, Llull wished to cover all comprehensible knowledge of God's mysteries. He realized the enormity of the task, comparing his burden to that of an ant carrying a heavier weight than its own body, and asked God for assistance (*OE,* 2:650). He began book 1 cheerfully: man must be joyful that God exists and created him and fellow humans. Llull then divided the subject matter of the five books as follows: book 1 deals with the divine attributes; book 2, God's providence and universe, including man; book 3, the nature of man; book 4, the articles of faith; and book 5, love and prayer.

Llibre de contemplació has puzzled critics who have tried to specify its genre, for it has both an encyclopedic character and an ascetic-mystical intention. At best it must be described as a mixed genre. Attempts to relate it to mystical works have not proved convincing; however, Llull must have used Augustine's *Confessions* as a literary model.[14] Also, his work contains autobiographical information and essential ideas he developed in later works.

In chapters 110–22 of book 3, Llull introduced a digression from the doctrinal content by discussing several professions and states: priests, princes, knights, pilgrims, judges and lawyers, doctors, merchants, sailors, *jongleurs,* shepherds, painters, farmers, and skilled workers. He used more structured and detailed prose to depict the *jongleurs,* painters, and sailors. His evaluation of each profession was influenced by his recent conversion. Therefore, he saw the clergy in a favorable light, while he drew kings, *jongleurs,* knights, lawyers, and physicians in the darkest hues, reflecting his disdain for the courtly ambience. His social criticism indicates analytic skill and perspicacity.

Llull's poetic prose surfaces especially in his comparisons. For example, the hazards threatening a ship at sea are like a mystic's temptations: "Humble Lord, full of mercy, the ships which endure bad weather at sea do not have the tempest and tribulations within them. These come rather from the wind and sea. But my ship, Lord, is in the tempest of tribulation, both from within and from without, for my physical sense torments my ship on its exterior, and my spiritual senses on the interior" (*OE,* 2:354). He also preferred the Lord's creation to the work of court painters: "We see artists, Lord, who paint the palaces, chambers, porches, and houses of princes in gold, silver, and other colors. But your palace and room in this world has no paint but the sun, wind, and rain. For your sole dwelling is outside of palaces and chambers, in the space between heaven and earth" (*OE,* 2:361).

A late medieval work on mysticism and philosophy, *Llibre de contemplació* offers a glimpse of the lyricism and technique Llull attained in *Blaquerna* and in *Felix.* Although it lacks images and a narrative framework, *Llibre de contemplació* is a masterpiece of Catalan literature because of its magnitude, diversity, depth, and sincerity of its author.

Llull wrote *Llibre del Gentil e dels tres savis* (Book of the Gentile and the three wise men) early in his career, perhaps as a manual of instruction for his Miramar missionary school.[15] He was fond of this work because it contained the "ten conditions of the tree," the foundation for his apologetic aims.[16] A reference in his prologue to "following the manner of the Arabic Book of the Gentile" has led to the belief that he either composed it originally in Arabic or used an Arabic source (*SW,* 1:93–94).

In *Llibre del Gentil* a pagan philosopher is plunged into a depression, for he believes neither in God nor an afterlife. This Gentile leaves his

country and comes upon an allegorical forest filled with wonders from
the plant and animal worlds. Meanwhile, three sages—a Jew, a Christian,
and a Muslim—who are spending a day in the country, enter a meadow
and see a spring that waters five trees. Near the spring, a beautiful
maiden, Intelligence, explains the significance of the trees and their
flowers, each of which contains a letter of the alphabet. The first tree,
which sprouts twenty-one flowers, represents the Lord and his uncreated
virtues; the second has forty-nine flowers, on which are written the
seven virtues of the first tree and the seven virtues leading to salvation;
the third has forty-nine, the seven created virtues and seven deadly sins;
the forth has twenty-one, the seven created virtues; the fifth has forty-
nine, the seven created virtues and seven mortal sins. No contradiction
can exist among the flowers. The knowledge of these trees and of virtue
will comfort the heathens and bring them to salvation. At this point
the maiden departs and the Gentile enters to refresh himself in the
spring.

After the three sages greet him, he informs them that he is a stranger
seeking consolation. When the sages realize he does not believe in an
afterlife, they agree—on his request—to prove the existence of God
and the Resurrection by means of the five trees and their flowers. The
Gentile believes their lessons and is overjoyed at God's existence and
an afterlife. However, realizing that the sages hold diverse creeds and
condemn the unacceptable beliefs of one another, his joy turns into
despair.

To console him the three wise men agree to debate the truths of
their religion. He asks them to debate according to the antiquity of
their respective faiths: Judaism, Christianity, and Islam. Thus, in book
2 the Jew explains the eight articles of his faith; in book 3 the Christian
discusses the fourteen articles of Christianity, emphasizing the Trinity
and Christ's humility; in book 4 the Muslim reveals beliefs taken from
the Koran.[17] After these presentations, the Gentile thanks God for
having enlightened him but does not declare what religion he has
chosen. Confident he will choose their religion, the sages leave him.[18]
Before they return to the city, they beg one another's pardon for offensive
remarks they may have made inadvertently and agree to continue their
discussions using speculative arguments until all have reached one faith,
an ideal throughout this work.

To present apologetic arguments according to his Art, Llull began
his prologue and first chapter in a simple language and style. This
literary simplicity entices the reader into the abstract reasoning of his

Art, according to Bonner (*SW,* 1:97–98), who found the logic of the Art more interesting in books 1 and 3 and sociological considerations more appealing in books 2 and 4. In several other works Llull cited and recommended this fundamental book to readers.[19] During the centuries after his death, it became one of his most popular works; translations appeared in Latin, Spanish, French, and possibly Hebrew. No doubt his literary skills, treatment of the three faiths, and ideal of religious unity account for its vogue.

Using two guidelines, Christianity and the Art, Llull wrote *Llibre de l'Orde de Cavalleria (Book of the Order of Chivalry)* between 1279 and 1283. Besides the themes and techniques of previous works (*locus amoenus,* allegory, comparison and contrast of opposites), Llull addressed his reader directly and personified virtues and vices, for example, Lust and Fortitude (part 6), which confront one another. The narrative begins in the prologue: an elderly knight returns to his hermitage, a place in Llull's works analogous to the *locus amoenus,* to live the rest of his life as a hermit. While at prayer, he sees a sleeping squire, providentially carried to his retreat, approaching on a horse. Having awakened, he informs the hermit that he is on his way to court to be made a knight. Hearing the squire's motive, the elder reflects, and realizing that the squire has little knowledge of the knight's responsibilities, offers him a short book on chivalry—the book Llull is writing. The squire accepts the volume and agrees to furnish copies to the new knights at court. Before parting he agrees to return, which he never does.

Llull divided *Llibre de l'Orde de Cavalleria* into seven parts, which signify the seven planets. Part 1 on the origins of knighthood is especially balanced due to the contrast of opposites established throughout: clergy / knighthood, love / fear, knowledge / arms. Llull sustained this balance by elaborating upon the requisites of chivalry. Part 2 deals with the knight's duties: to defend and uphold the Catholic faith, to protect his terrestrial ruler, to defend the weak and innocent, and to maintain peace. In part 3, which describes a test the squire must take to enter knighthood, Llull reiterated the ideal of justice and the requirement of nobility.[20] Part 4, mostly given to Christian doctrine, relates the ceremony of knighthood. Part 5 continues the clergy / knight parallel and deals with the symbolism of the knight's armor—a medieval topos—comparing these arms to the traditional interpretation of the priest's vestments. Part 6 discusses the moral principles of knighthood, stressing justice (the just medium and the common good) and prudence. The last part enumerates the honor due to the knight.

The function and status of knighthood changed significantly from the ninth to the thirteenth century, when it took on a more mundane character. Llull wished to change this secular status of knighthood with his *Llibre de l'Orde de Cavalleria,* in which he emphasized the main duties of knighthood: to serve God and maintain order. Therefore, his book on chivalry became a code to transform nobles into knights of Christ. To complete this change, Llull transformed the knight's world into a Utopia.[21]

Doctrina pueril (1282–83), a religious and practical manual Llull addressed to his son, Dominic, has a specific and general intention— to instruct Dominic and to inform parents and educators about educating youth. Its one hundred chapters show a division in content and proceed from the general to the particular: (1) religious and doctrinal principles; (2) moral and secular education. In these chapters Llull covers a wide field of knowledge, for example, the origin and propagation of Judaism, Christianity, and Islam (chaps. 68–72); princes and clergy (80–81); the four elements, free will, the Antichrist, the seven ages of the world, angels, hell, and heaven (94–100). In short, the subject matter, didactic content, and ideals (missionary zeal and religious unification) make *Doctrina pueril* one of Llull's typical works.

This compact encyclopedia is important because few practical peda-gogical works were written in the late Middle Ages, especially in the vernacular.[22] When compared to contemporary works of the same genre, such as Vincent de Beauvais's *Liber de eruditione puerorum regalium* (Book on the instruction of the king's children), Llull's primer seems original in content and style. For example, he contended that the son of nobles should learn a trade, a Moorish practice, which is absent in similar European works. Llull also advised children to begin learning to read and write in their native tongue at a time when Latin dominated European learning.

Llull often structured the chapter content according to a logical plan: he announced the subject in general terms, developed its theme by examples and related topics, and drew conclusions leading to the mention of God. He used short, rhythmic sentences and simple images because he intended the book for his son's reading. At times, however, the logical argumentation seems beyond an adolescent's comprehension and interest, particularly the passage on knowledge given by the Holy Spirit and the dialectic on homicide.[23]

Written in Montpellier about 1290, *Llibre de sancta Maria* (Book of Saint Mary), a mystical work set into an allegorical framework, deals with Mariology, one of Llull's favorite themes. It generally follows the structure of *Llibre del Gentil*, in which the narrative frames the body of the work, but becomes a series of conversations between a hermit and three ladies—Prayer, Praise, and Intention—about the thirty attributes of Mary. Prayer and Praise meet on a well-traveled path and lament the lack of devotion and their frail and pallid condition. They journey through the allegorical forest and come upon Intention, who, at the thought of sinfulness, tears her garment and dishevels her hair. The three walk to a hermitage dedicated to Mary, where they meet an unlearned hermit, who directs them to the hermitage of a saintly and learned man (perhaps a representation of Llull himself). Upon learning their identities, the learned hermit sits with them to discuss the attributes of Mary, the subject of the rest of the work.

The conversation follows a rigid structure: the hermit asks Praise to define the attributes of Mary discussed in the chapter; two *semblances* (images or metaphors) given by the hermit and Intention, respectively, reinforce this definition. Prayer, whose intensity contrasts with the tranquillity of Praise, addresses the attribute under consideration; the hermit and Intention again recount one *semblança* each. The numerous *semblances* often relate a miracle of Mary, which differ from others in medieval works because of their temporal vagueness and paradigmatic structure.[24] Like the *exempla,* these miracles are brief and undeveloped.

As a literary work, *Llibre de sancta Maria* is inferior to other allegorical works by Llull; in addition, its chapter organization seems, at times, unsystematic. On the other hand, this work should not be judged severely or on literary merits alone. Llull applied *Llibre de intenció* (ca. 1283) to Mary's virtues by examining them according to the first and second intention.[25] In this way he believed his reader would understand the *semblances* of this devotional and mystical work.

Llull divided *Blaquerna*[26] or *Llibre d'Evast e d'Aloma e de Blaquerna* (Book of Evast, Aloma, and Blaquerna, ca. 1283) into five parts, corresponding to the five wounds of Christ. The five sections also represent the individual's status: "The first is matrimony, the second of the religious life, the third of prelacy, the fourth of the apostolic estate of the Pope and his Cardinals, and the fifth of the life of the hermit."[27] After admitting a didactic motive for this division, Llull described an ideal mode of living for each status.

Except for the early chapters, the work revolves around Blaquerna, the only child of Evast, a merchant, and Aloma, a noble, both humble servants of God. When Blaquerna completes his education, they decide to leave him their wealth and lead a religious life. They inform him of their plans only to find out that he too wishes to live a hermit's life. Aloma schemes to have Blaquerna speak to her neighbor's daughter, Natana, whose youth and beauty, she hopes, will persuade him to marry. But the plan goes awry: Blaquerna persuades Natana to enter the convent. Convinced that they cannot change his plans Evast and Aloma follow their son to a forest and take leave of him, knowing they will never see him again. The remainder of book 1 describes how Evast and Aloma gradually give all their possessions to the poor and lead beggars' lives. In book 2 Natana enters the convent and becomes a sacristan and eventually the abbess.

In chapter 42 Blaquerna, who begins his journey through the allegorical forest in search of a hermitage, lives two fantastic adventures, both skillfully written: the Ten Commandments and Valor. In the latter episode a jester and the emperor, both unworthy to enter the palace of Lady Valor, must accompany Blaquerna. The three episodes that follow are among the most psychologically developed creations of *Blaquerna:* the consolation of the shepherd whose son was eaten by wolves; the rescue of the maiden and Blaquerna's subsequent temptation to sin with her; and the conversion of the knight, Sir Narpan. Now Blaquerna becomes a monk and shortly after is elected abbot, a position that allows him to begin monastic reform. In book 3, Blaquerna becomes a bishop and introduces diocesan reforms according to the eight Beatitudes. Llull's literary talent surfaces here in the action and dialogue of anecdotes surrounding the canons representing the Beatitudes, especially Persecution, who frequents taverns to convert their clients and confronts dishonest cloth merchants.

In book 4 Blaquerna ascends the Church hierarchy and becomes pope. In this, the most utopian section of *Blaquerna,* Llull contrasts his own idealistic reforms with the problems of contemporary pontiffs. He includes in the papal court the Jongeur of Valor and Ramon the Fool, Llull himself (ca. 43), who add greater diversity to his narrative and to the mystical content. The two characters intermingle in the early chapters of book 4 by singing praises to the beloved and narrating *exempla,* which convince Blaquerna of necessary reform in the papal court. Cardinals, each of whom has an office named after a phrase in the Gloria of the Mass, undertake the reform. Here Llull stressed several ideas he pursued throughout his apostolic life: missionary zeal, pedagogical reform, conversion of infidels, and religious and linguistic unity— Catholicism and Latin being preferred. In book 5 the cardinals reluctantly allow Blaquerna to resign the papacy. To seclude himself in prayer and contemplation, he retires to a nearby hermitage, where he writes *Llibre d'Amic e Amat (Book of the Lover and the Beloved)* and *Art de contemplació (Art of Contemplation).*

In the brief epilogue Blaquerna asks a penitent jester to read *Blaquerna* in public. Also, the emperor of book 2 returns to the papal court and, when told of Blaquerna's whereabouts, sets out to find him. Llull does not inform the reader if the emperor encountered the holy man, preferring instead to underscore the renunciation by both ecclesiastical and temporal leaders for the Lord's sake.

Religious reform preoccupied Llull, especially in 1310, when he sought aid from Prince Philip of Mallorca, who was influenced by the Spiritual Angelo Clareno. Llull expressed his discontent with worldly clerics at the Council of Vienne and in works such as *Petitio in concilio generali,* advocating measures to curb clerical opulence and *Phantasticus* (Fantastic). He also urged that the Church promote moral changes, believing that once Christians began living Christ's life, the peaceful and apostolic conquest of the world was inevitable. To foster this ideal Llull animated several characters, especially the canons of book 3, with the Franciscan spirit of love, renunciation, and poverty.

Blaquerna embodies the Christian ideal of perfection and lives out Llull's own fantasies. Also, characters such as Ramon the Fool, the Jongleur of Valor, and the adolescent Blaquerna present glimpses of Llull's own personality and life. Minor personages reflect his social, moral, and religious beliefs. In short, Llull transforms the society in which he lives into the Utopia for which he longs.

In order to gather a large audience, Llull concentrated on the narrative structure of *Blaquerna.* To give his lay readers the knowledge of his Art and reformist beliefs, he chose a literary form similar to that of the *roman.*[28] Also, he incorporated in *Blaquerna exempla* and Arabic fables, selecting them to correspond to the main narrative and structuring their content in a tightly written prose.[29] He also drew allegorical characters (Ten Commandments, Faith, Truth, Understanding, Devotion) with greater character and emotion than those from *Llibre del Gentil* and *Llibre de sancta Maria,* and had them engage in animated dialogue. Llull included several shorter works within *Blaquerna,* the first of which, *Llibre de Ave Maria* (bk. 2, chaps. 61–66), is divided according to the six parts of the prayer, "Ave Maria," and contains praises, anecdotes, and legends of Mary. Written by the abbot Blaquerna, this devotional reveals decadence and extols Llull's reformist ideas for cenobite life.

Blaquerna represents an early step in European narrative development. Because of its mature narrative technique and originality, it is a key work of medieval prose literature. It also contains *Llibre d'Amic e Amat,* Llull's best example of poetic prose, and another mystical work, *Art de contemplació.* Llull wrote the first work (366 short paragraphs for daily reading) in simple prose with internal rhyme and dialogue between the Lover (the Christian), the Beloved (the Creator or Christ), and Love (the personification of love that exists between the two): " 'Say, O Lover!' asked the Beloved, 'If I double thy trial, wilt thou still be patient?' 'Yea,' answered the Lover, 'so that Thou double also my love' " (*B,* 413, no. 9).

Llull probably wrote this short devotional work between 1276 and 1283 at Miramar and used it as the lengthy chapter 98 of *Blaquerna.*[30] After Blaquerna retires to his hermitage, fellow hermits ask him to write a book to teach contemplation and devotion to other hermits. The hero complies after contemplating God.

Llull used a subtle method so that the reader must reflect on the meaning of each meditation. Delicate images reflect the Lover's unity to the Beloved, such as the following, common among the troubadours: "Love is an ocean; its waves are troubled by the winds; it has no port or shore. The Lover perished in the ocean, and with him perished his torments, and the work of his fulfilment began" (*B,* 447, no. 235).

Llull personified abstract ideas as in the following dialogue among contraries:

Love and Indifference met in a garden, where the Lover and the Beloved were talking in secret. And Love asked Indifference for what intent he had come to that place. "That the Lover may cease to love," he replied, "and the Beloved to be honoured." The words of Indifference were greatly displeasing to the Beloved and the Lover, and their love was increased, that it might vanquish and destroy Indifference. (*B,* 435–36, no. 163)

Through a series of paradoxes and antitheses reversing the practical values of life, Llull conveys the Lover's desire for unity with the Beloved: the greater the Lover's torment, the greater his tranquillity and the stronger his condition (nos. 50, 87, 243): the sorrow for the Beloved brings happiness (no. 65); poverty is his wealth (nos. 56, 201); fear is not being with the Beloved (nos. 119, 121); the paths to the Beloved are both long and short (no. 69); loneliness is the companionship of people (nos. 46–47); the Lover fears falling asleep, for his only rest is the sorrow and torments of his waking hours: "The Lover was fain to sleep, for he had laboured much in seeking his Beloved; and he feared lest he should forget Him. And he wept, that he might not fall asleep, and his Beloved be absent from his remembrance" (B, 415, no. 28). The meditations represent a variety of structures and styles, attained at times through exclamation (no. 127), apostrophe (nos. 35, 73–74, 299–300), or a series of brief and rapid questions and answers (nos. 79, 97). Llull also used metaphors common to mystical writers: the cloud between Lover and Beloved, the ladder of ascent, the ocean of love. However, the hermit's poetic meditations comparing nature to the mystical experience are among the most lyrical passages:

The birds hymned the dawn, and the Lover, who is the dawn, awakened. And the birds ended their song, and the Lover died in the dawn for his Beloved. (B, 415, no. 26)

The Lover came to drink of the fountain which gives love to him that has none, and his grief redoubled. And the Beloved came to drink of that fountain, that the love of one whose grief were doubled might be doubled also. (B, 414, no. 22)

Llibre d'Amic e Amat is both didactic and philosophical. Into it Llull incorporated theological beliefs such as the Trinity (nos. 50, 166, 211), the Incarnation (no. 371), and the Last Judgment (no. 353). Psychologically, Llull described in poetic terms the three powers of the soul—memory, understanding, and will—relating these to his own experiences. A knowledge of these powers is essential to understanding this devotional, as Arthur Terry suggests:

A modern reader may be inclined to see the Libre d'Amic e Amat as a series of disconnected prose fragments interspersed with more abstract reflections. . . . There are very few verses, in fact, which do not refer in one way or another to the operation of the three powers of the soul . . . ; if one reads the book in this way, one finds that every verse contributes, separately and in combination, to a single total pattern which conveys the essense of Llull's theological speculations.[31]

Llull used images from the real world (birds, ocean, flowers, dawn) in the first two thirds of his meditations. However, in the last hundred he preferred abstract concepts and plays on words. Although the meditations seem unrelated and obscure, Llull provided the reader with the means to interpret them, as Robert Pring-Mill has shown.[32]

Scholars have had difficulty identifying the sources of *Llibre d'Amic e Amat* because of Llull's tone and synthetic talent. Although *Song of Songs,* the Franciscan mystics—Bonaventure and Jacopone da Todi—and the troubadours affected parts of this devotional, it may owe its principal inspiration to Arabic sources, for Llull himself wrote that when Blaquerna considered the manner in which to write his meditations, "he remembered . . . that the Saracens . . . have certain men called Sufi, who . . . have words of love and brief examples which give to men great devotion" (*B,* 410).[33]

Blaquerna has a circular structure (Blaquerna fulfills his youthful desire to become a hermit in the final chapters). The narrative also progresses vertically toward the Utopia which the hermit Blaquerna finds. However, Blaquerna fulfills Llull's purpose for writing this romance not by becoming a hermit but by living as a contemplative, an experience that involves reading, meditating on, and experiencing thoughts of his *Llibre d'Amic e Amat* in order to become the Lover. Therefore, this work represents an essential part of *Blaquerna.*[34]

The hermit Blaquerna also wrote *Art de contemplació,* a systematic presentation of Llull's mystical doctrine. The thirteen parts of the former work, essentially meditations of the divine virtues, relate to one another or to the other parts of this didactic manual and address the following themes: essence, unity, Trinity, Incarnation, the *Our Father, Ave Maria,* Ten Commandments, *Miserere,* sacraments, other virtues, and vices. The mystic Blaquerna seeks companionship by personifying the abstractions he discusses: theological and cardinal virtues, powers of the soul, and Remembrance. In its content and simple language and style, *Art de contemplació* complements the larger work of which it forms an important part. Compared to Llull's earlier speculative works, this mystical manual shows his talent for presenting speculative and doctrinal knowledge in clear, poetic language.

Llull wrote *Llibre de meravelles* (Book of wonders), which also was named after its main character *Felix,* in Paris around 1288 and 1289, a time when he was "sad and melancholy" (*SW,* 2:659).[35] In it he combined thirteenth-century natural and scientific knowledge with religious, social, and political beliefs, divided into ten parts or books (God, angels, the heavens, elements, plants, metals, beasts, man, paradise, hell) joined together by an episodic narrative focused on young Felix.

The ten-part division is often uneven, as book 8, on man, takes up almost three fifths of the work, and book 3 contains only two chapters. Felix's father commissions him to "travel through the world and wonder why men no longer love and know God" (*SW*, 2:659). Felix then leaves his father and enters the great forest, where he undergoes the first of three temptations, all of which cause him to doubt God's existence, a major theme.[36] Learned hermits, including Blaquerna (who appears briefly), instruct the youth on the supernatural and natural world. Felix continues his long pilgrimage through towns, cities, and palaces, speaking to people from every social strata, and questioning each wonder he witnesses. His answers come in the form of *exempla* or in didactic passages.

Although in *Felix* Llull included themes, motifs, and techniques he had used several years before in *Blaquerna*, the differences between these two works reveal his motive for writing *Felix*.[37] He developed *Blaquerna* biographically, whereas in *Felix* he stressed its didacticism. Felix questions hermits about a world he does not understand. In return he receives extensive knowledge of the world. Llull therefore gave *Felix* an encyclopedic character to expound his Art, and this knowledge often comes in *exempla* and stories that Llull narrated from medieval sources and his own experience. In them he offered simple arguments, often loosely connected, that form an essential part of *Felix*.

Llull made the prologue and section 107 of book 8, "Intention," a fundamental part of *Felix:* "God created the world with the intention of being loved and known by man. . . . Most men, however, do not follow the purpose for which they were created, but rather act as if they were created for some other purpose, or in other words, they think they were created to be loved and known, honored, and served" (*SW*, 2:1048). Therefore, according to Llull's belief in first and second intentions, man had made the second intention his first, thereby confusing God's reason for begetting man and bringing about a world upside down. Llull, however, was not content with specifying the cause of evil; he proposed solutions, introducing social criticism in *Felix*. Blaming rulers for social ills, Llull insisted that they and all men, through reason, accept God's first and second creative intention. In addition, he promoted, through dialogues with hermits and shepherds, a return to primitive society. At the end of the work, Felix dies, but a "second Felix" fulfills his unaccomplished mission, to go "throughout the world recounting [*Llibre de meravelles*], and adding to it, according to the wonders he encountered" (*SW*, 2:1105).

Felix contains one outstanding section, book 7, entitled "Llibre de les bèsties" ("Book of Beasts"), in which Felix hears the allegory about animals, beginning with the election of a king, in which the herbivores oppose the carnivores.[38] Dame Reynard, a deceptive fox, plots to have the lion elected king. The leaders of the opposition, the ox and the horse, abandon the animal kingdom to join the kingdom of man, only to be deceived and abused. Man yokes the ox and harnesses the horse, and when the ox realizes he will be fattened and eaten, both animals leave their tyrannical superior. The leopard and the lynx are then sent to the king of man bearing gifts of the cat and the dog, but find him ungrateful, lascivious, and immoral. Upon their return the leopard learns that the lion has seduced his spouse and must avenge his honor in battle with the king's representative, the lynx. The leopard wins the fight but is killed by the lion. Therefore, through plotting and deceit, Dame Reynard gradually eliminates the strong beasts on the king's council, replacing them with small, timid ones. When she conspires to overthrow the king of beasts, the elephant reveals the plot to the lion, who kills Dame Reynard, and peace returns to the animal kingdom.

Llull carefully chose his sources, especially *Roman de Renard,*[39] *Kalila and Dimna,* and, to a lesser extent *Sendebar* and *Thousand and One Nights,* selectively changed them, and added new elements, such as the election of the lion.[40] As a result, the "Llibre de les bèsties" is a more concentrated narrative within *Felix* and a powerful satire on human ambitions, and especially on bad policies of kings. Llull artfully criticized man's vices through the animals who describe his immortality and ingratitude, often through fables. He also satirized the person of low social status (Dame Reynard) who, through intrigue and manipulations, attempts to rise in the court. Such individuals cannot behave honorably: "My lord," said the elephant, "not much wine can fit in a small goblet, nor can great honor or great loyalty be present in someone of vile origin" (*SW,* 2:823).

Llull wrote "Llibre de les bèsties" in a simple language, rapid dialogue, and unpretentious style. Also, some of its episodes show his talent for creating unified, effective narratives, such as the election of the lion, or simple stories, such as the tale of the kite and the rat (*SW,* 2:788–89). Although its themes refer directly to the message of *Felix,* "Llibre de les bèsties" has often been published separately in Catalan or in translation. Because of its unified structure and unique tone within *Felix,* it reads well as a separate work. Llull encouraged the impression of this work as a satire on rulers and a manual for instructing princes, by having Felix present it to a king in order to inform him about how to rule and to guard against evil advisors.

In Rome from 29 September 1295 to 1 April 1296, Llull wrote another work, encyclopedic in character, *Arbre de sciència* (Tree of science), in order to make his Art accessible to a larger segment of readers. Therefore, *Arbre de sciència* reveals the content of *Art generalis ultima,* which he explained in simple, nontechnical terms. Llull used sixteen trees as a frame for the doctrinal content: elemental (cosmology and metaphysics), vegetal (botany, medicine), sensual (zoology), imaginal (impressions and their application to the mechanical and liberal arts), human (anthropology and psychology), moral (ethics), imperial (political science), apostolic (Church governance), celestial (astrology and astronomy), angelical (angelology), eviternal (escatology), maternal (Mariology), Christian (Christology), divine (theology), exemplary (illustrates previous sections with examples useful in preaching), and interrogative (resolves questions pertaining to previous sections). The last two sections or trees form an appendix to the first fourteen. Llull further selected a seven-part division for each tree: (roots, trunk, branches, boughs, leaves, flowers, fruit). However, the divided parts taken together form a unified hierarchal structure to explain each division of knowledge.[41]

In part 15, "Arbre exemplifical" (Exemplary tree), Llull provided examples from nature and the growth of trees, examples that he divided into two groups: *recontaments* (apologues) and *proverbis* (proverbs).[42] However, the distinction between the two is unclear, for, according to Jordi Rubió i Balaguer, they are all short sayings with a didactic purpose.[43] In this, the most literary section of *Arbre de sciència,* Llull personified the four elements, powers of the soul, animals, celestial bodies, seasons, geometric shapes, abstract concepts, and virtues, all of which interact in animated dialogue with poetry and humor:

Springtime scolded the Sun for having destroyed in the summer the beautiful wonders it had created in April and May. (*OE,* 1:804)

The donkey told his master that he knew how to sing, and the master told him that he knew how to cry. (*OE,* 1:806)

Other sections of "Arbre exemplifical" contain *exempla* and miracles of Mary, for example, the account of Honor and the peasant in the "apostolic bough" or of the Church and the bishop in the "angelical branch." Llull also introduced rapid dialogue and rhymed prose in the proverbs, including the dialogue of the rose and the pepper.[44]

Tree of Love (1298), which represents "the final moment in the development of Llull's doctrine of love,"[45] began with the disappointments and frustrations he experienced, which made him leave Paris and set out for a nearby forest to meditate and plan this allegorical work. There Llull meets a lady, Philosophy-of-Love, who jealously complains that her sister, Philosophy-of-Knowledge, has more followers, for men forget to love when they master knowledge. He consoles her with the information that he has composed *Ars amativa boni* (Art of loving good) (1290) and will begin *Tree of Love.*

The story of the first of two lovers begins in section 5. We accompany the first Lover through his sighs, tears, and fears (the three leaves of the tree). The Lover becomes ill, and the Physician of Love gives him medicine made from the roots of the tree of love "that it might be very potent."[46] The medicine and its antidote add to his frenzy and sickness of love and cause the Lover to flee. He is captured and imprisoned, tried, and condemned to death by the Beloved. Consoled at the Lover's death, the Lady of Love is allowed to choose another Lover in part 6, the flowers of love, a long series of epigrams on the glories, praises, and honors of love. The Lover, the Ladies of Love, and the Servitors of Love agree to go through the world so that the Beloved may be "known, loved, honoured and served by all" (*Tree of Love,* 93). Later, a pilgrim reproves their decision to leave the world and encourages them to continue their lives in society to serve and love the Beloved. The last section, the fruits of love, contains questions in which the Servitors of Love attempt to prove the worth of the Lover, who, unlike the first Lover, is loyal and confident.

Llull combined the lyricism of *Llibre d'Amic e Amat* with the tenets of the Art enumerated in *Ars amativa;* he also incorporated images and allegory from Provençal models, for example, the death-from-love allegory, into the symbolism of the Tree. He also reintroduced his seven-part division of the Tree, used in *Arbre de sciència,* with modifications: there is one tree with roots divided into eighteen categories. Although not a mystical work in the strict sense, it has been called a "philosophical and literary exposition of mystical love."[47]

In *Tree of Love* Llull again explained his Art using a literary frame and his theory of love of God. Although he constructed a firm structure for this work, its seven parts seem unevenly divided. Its images sometimes lack the vitality of those in *Llibre d'Amic e Amat.*[48] Yet despite these shortcomings, Llull brought forth in *Tree of Love* an allegory expressing the essence and culmination of his philosophy of love.

His Influence

Lullism.[49]   Llull's influence has been partial and, at times, indirect, a circumstance that Joan Triadú attributes to Llull's individualism and the failure of subsequent thinkers to realize the full importance of his reasoning.[50] Although Lullism has never received the attention accorded to Thomism, Scottism, and other medieval philosophies, it had followers from the fourteenth to the eighteenth century. These followers usually became interested in one or two facets of Llull's thought: the Art, logic, mysticism, ethics, or anti-Averroist views. His legendary reputation as an alchemist brought about seventy-seven alchemical works written spuriously under his name (*SW*, 1:73–74). Also, his fame as a Cabalist, which has its origin in another spurious work, *De auditu cabbalistico* (Caballist report), caught the attention of Pico della Mirandola (1463–94) and Giordano Bruno (1548–1600).

The activities of Llull's disciples, especially Thomas le Myésier (d. 1336), and the opposition taken by Nicholas Eymerich (1302–99), and Jean Gerson (1363–1429), characterize the early history of Lullism. Le Myésier became a liaison between two centers of Lullism: the Sorbonne and Vauvert. His four Lullian compilations, two of which have survived (*Electorium* and *Breviculum*), represent his main contribution to continuing Llull's thought.[51] Eymerich and Gerson opposed Llull's supposed rationalism, an opposition motivated perhaps by a new nominalist movement that took place at Paris during their time.[52]

In the fifteenth century, the Lullian schools of Barcelona and Mallorca spread his thought to Italy, especially to Padua and Venice. At the same time, Nicholas de Cusa (1401–64) began collecting and editing Llull's works at Kues, perhaps because of his interest in Llull's mystical doctrine.[53] The Catalan Ramon Sibiuda (d. 1436), whose writings were admired by Montaigne and Pascal, became interested in the Art, as did Pico della Mirandola, who tried to harmonize the Art with the Cabala (*SW*, 1:74, 77–79).

Through his publications of Llull's mystical works, Jacques Lefevre d'Etaples (ca. 1455–1536) and his disciples began new European interest in Llull, which reached its height in the sixteenth and seventeenth centuries. However, Pere Daguí of the Mallorcan school must be credited with renewing Lullism in Spain and Italy. He prepared editions of

Llull's works that appeared in Seville, Barcelona, and Rome; also, his trip to Rome (1485) led to interest in Llull's Art, which gradually reached his first German commentator, Henry Cornelius Agrippa (1486–1535).[54]

Llull's influence also spread in fourteenth- and fifteenth-century Castile as evidenced by his works housed in Castilian libraries and Spanish translations, such as the *Llibre del Gentil,* which was translated in 1378. His reputation also continued among Hispanic Beguines and Spirituals, and his Art and doctrinal ideas affected *Libro de Gonzalo Morante.*[55] After the Catholic kings and the Hapsburgs came to power, Llull's influence spread through Spain. Cardinal Cisneros introduced his thought at the University of Alcalá, helped to publish and catalog his works, and established a library of Lullian studies. Philip II of Spain gathered a library of his works at the Escorial, established an academy in Madrid to promote philosophy and mathematics, including Lullism, and encouraged his canonization. His son Philip III continued his interest in Llull. And in 1673 a chair of Lullian studies at the University of Mallorca received papal approval.

A revival of Lullism occurred in Germany and France during the last half of the sixteenth century and culminated with Giordano Bruno's seven commentaries on the Art. In addition, Lazarus Zetzner included four of Bruno's commentaries in his anthologies, which influenced Leibniz's early work, *Dissertatio de arte combinatoria* (Dissertation on the combinatory Art, 1666). Descartes may have also consulted Llull before he conceived his new method of constituting a universal science.[56]

Lullism declined in the Age of Enlightenment despite the efforts of Ivo Salzinger (1669–1728), editor of the Mainz edition of Llull's works, who defended alchemical works attributed to Llull and their application at a time when alchemy had lost prestige. During the same period in Spain, Lullism grew, despite attacks by the essayist Benito Jerónimo Feijóo (1676–1764), which were countered by several Spaniards.[57] Antonio Raymundo Pasqual (1708–91) led the attack with his *Vindiciae lullianae* (Defense of Llull), published in 1778.

Literary Influence. Llull exerted significant influence, especially on Hispanic literature. European authors used *Llibre de l'Orde de Cavalleria* as a popular model and sterotyped his concept of the knight. Don Juan Manuel may have used the opening of Llull's treatise as a model for his *Libro del cavallero e del escudero* (Book of the knight and the squire), although missing pages from the Spanish text make it difficult to assess the extent of the influence.[58] Don Juan Manuel may have also read *Llibre del Gentil* and *Blaquerna* and incorporated the doctrinal ideas of the former and the sociopolitical thought of the latter into his *Libro de los Estados* (Book on the plan of society). The Valencian Joanot Martorell, author of the Catalan classic *Tirant lo Blanc,* wrote an earlier unfinished work entitled *Guillem de Varoic,* an adaptation of *Roman de Gui de Wárwick* (Romance of Guy of Warwick) combined with the structural and doctrinal frame of *Llibre de l'Orde de Cavalleria.* He subsequently incorporated the *Guillem de Varoic* into the opening chapter of the *Tirant* (*OE,* 1:524).

Numerous translations and editions dating from the fifteenth century attest to the popularity of *Llibre de l'Orde de Cavalleria.* In 1456 Gilbert Haye translated it into Scots based on a French version. William Caxton's English translation appeared about 1484 at Westminster,[59] ten years before a new Scots translation by Adam Loutfut, and fostered the courtly ideal of Elizabethan England.[60]

Llull's concepts, style, mystical thought, and metaphysics influenced the Spanish mystics. In his mystical works Llull transmitted the heritage he received from the *Sufi* to mystics of the early sixteenth century and Spanish Golden Age. More specifically, he brought to the mystics from the *Sufi* the concepts of the affective union, the idea of pure, disinterested love, and the symbol of the knot, which Theresa of Avila employed. Theresa and John of the Cross also used Llull's image of the mirror-font, another Arabic derivation. Llull, Theresa, and John of the Cross also stressed particular characteristics of the mystical process.[61] Finally, the poetic content of Llull's work affected one of the leading Catalan poets, Jacint Verdaguer (1845–1902), who before his own death was compiling a study of Llull's *Llibre d'Amic e Amat.*[62]

Chapter Three
Arnau de Vilanova
Biography

Arnau de Vilanova was born around 1238 probably in Valencia.[1] Little is known about his early schooling except that he mastered Latin and Arabic in addition to his native Catalan.

About 1260 Arnau began medical studies at the University of Montpellier, possibly continuing his training in Naples. Like many medieval physicians, he became a cleric, though his marriage prevented his advancement in the Church. In 1281 he entered the court in Barcelona as the doctor of Peter II, and after Peter's death he served as royal physician of Peter's sons Alphonse II (1285–91) and James II (1285–1327).

From 1289 to 1299, Arnau taught at the University of Montpellier, where he helped improve the medical curriculum. He also became interested in the prophetic-apocalyptic ideas of Joachim of Flora and Peter John Olivi, and under their influence wrote an introduction to *De semine scripturarum* (On the seed of scriptures) in 1292, a commentary on Joachite beliefs, and *De adventu antichristi et fine mundi* (On the coming of the Antichrist and the end of the world), a prediction of the Antichrist's appearance in 1345.

Arnau left Montpellier in 1299 to represent James II on a diplomatic mission to Philip IV of France. His heterodox escatological ideas angered the theological faculty at the Sorbonne, which condemned his *De adventu antichristi,* denounced him, and recommended his imprisonment. In order to appease the theology faculty, Pope Boniface VIII forced Arnau to deny his escatological beliefs before the bishop of Paris and Parisian theologians.

In 1301 Arnau entered the papal court, where he cured Boniface VIII of a kidney problem. As a gratuity, he was given a summer vacation at the castle of Scurcola and an admonition: "Devote yourself to medicine and we will honor you."[2] He disregarded the pope's advice, however, by immediately writing another treatise *De cymbalis ecclesiae*

(The cymbals of the Church), in which he presented himself as God's prophet for Church reform.

After attending Queen Blanca d'Anjou in 1302, Arnau again became embroiled in controversy, especially with the Dominicans, and was finally excommunicated by the inquisitor Guillem de Cotlliure. A short time later his excommunication was revoked at James's insistence; Arnau then turned his attention to the Franciscan Spirituals.

Arnau left Valencia for Avignon around 1303 to attend the new pope, Benedict XI, another pontiff who needed medical services but who disapproved of Arnau's religious reforms. When Benedict died in 1304, Arnau along with a confrere, Bernat Deliciós, was suspected of poisoning the pope; however, he was never investigated.

In 1305 Arnau's friend Bertram de Got became Pope Clement V. Clement, however, neither approved of nor condemned Arnau's works. This papal indifference caused Arnau to lose interest in papal support and to seek aid from James II, Frederick III of Sicily (James's brother), and Robert of Naples.[3]

Having called Arnau to Barcelona, James told him about a strange and recurrent dream, in which his father, Peter II, had appeared to him. Arnau interpreted the dream according to his reformist beliefs and may have convinced James to begin a crusade against the Moors of Granada. Frederick III then beckoned Arnau to his court so that the physician could interpret a dream he had had intermittently for seven years. In this dream Frederick's mother appeared to him with her face covered and asked him to free himself from the service of truth. Arnau gave the same importance and interpretation to Frederick's dream that he had to his brother's and further identified the two monarchs with the Good Emperor in Jean de Roquetaillade's apocalyptic tradition, insisting that both kings would lead a Church reform.[4]

To gather support for a crusade, Arnau presented at Avignon a discourse, *Interpretatio de visionibus in somniis* (Interpretation of visions in dreams), in which he revealed and interpreted James's and Frederick's dreams. Informed of the discourse, James asked Arnau for a Catalan version of the speech. When the king realized that the account of the dreams had been omitted in the vernacular version, he broke immediately with his physician and encouraged Frederick to do the same. But Frederick, who had mystical tendencies and believed in the prophetic-apocalyptic tradition, welcomed Arnau, fellow Spirituals, and Beguines to Sicily. Arnau remained in Sicily, where he continued corresponding with James until 6 September 1311, when he died in a shipwreck off the Genovese coast.

His Beliefs and Influence

Although difficult to classify, Arnau's apocalyptic beliefs bear a direct relationship to those of Joachim of Flora.[5] The physician became more radical, however, as his opposition increased, finally acquiring the reputation as a prophet of doom and an anti-Scholastic.[6] Indeed, clerical degeneracy drove him to religious fanaticism and to a yearning for Church reform. He continued to predict the Antichrist's coming and the imminent end of the world so that people, especially the clergy, might sanctify themselves, overcome the final crisis, and defend Christ's cause. To achieve this ideal, Arnau advocated humility and the utopian Spiritualist life of abject poverty. His plan for reform and his blunt manner inevitably antagonized the clergy.

Arnau based his anticlericalism on his opposition to Scholasticism and to moral laxity among the clergy. Convinced of an imminent catastrophe, he blamed the relaxation of monastic ideals and clerical degeneracy for the impending crisis. Because the pope and papal court refused to impose religious and monastic reforms, he singled them out as the major cause of corruption. Lastly, as a true reformer, he took up the Bible, as interpreted by medieval visionaries, as his ultimate inspiration.

Arnau shunned Scholasticism, especially Thomism, because he wanted to return to primitive Christianity, a common ideal among the Franciscan Spirituals.[7] He believed Scholasticism contradicted the simplicity and spirit of the Bible, the New Testament in particular. He also opposed the origins of Scholasticism, especially Aristotelianism, which formed the basis for Thomist and Dominican thought, because he feared that Aristotle's pagan philosophy would overshadow Catholic dogma.[8] In Arnau's mind, a parallel and progressive secularization of dogma had in part caused the gradual secularization of society and the lack of Christian virtue. He opposed not only Aristotelianism but also all secular philosophies which, when applied to Christianity, encouraged rationalizing religious beliefs. As a result, Arnau began to polemize against the Dominicans, writing diatribes (for example, *Gladius iugalans Thomatistas* [Sword of truth against the Thomists]), and adhering to the Spirituals.[9]

Notwithstanding his violent attacks and brusque manner when presenting his beliefs, Arnau was not a revolutionary. He wished to reform the Church from within and believed that only the pope could effect the changes he envisioned. Only after three popes ignored his appeals for change did he insist that civil authority carry out social reform and conquer the heathen. Consequently, five years after Arnau's death, an assembly at Tarragona of laymen and religious banned his religious works. According to Menéndez y Pelayo, the fear of increased heterodoxy among the people and the spread of the ideals of Franciscan Spirituals and Beguines made condemning Arnau's vernacular works imminent. The Spanish Inquisition later condemned his works and destroyed his vernacular opuscules.

However, Arnau's influence continued in smaller religious circles. For example, a Beguine group in Tarragona and Franciscan Spirituals and Beguines in Provence and in Sicily remembered him and his reformist ideals. Also, Frederick III incorporated several of his political and social reforms into the Sicilian constitution of 15 October 1310.[10] As a result, Sicily became a temporary haven for Spirituals, especially after the Church and European monarchs condemned their beliefs. In later years, Arnau's religious works were translated into Spanish and may have influenced the Spanish Golden Age.[11]

Arnau's fame is also based on his medical knowledge and writings. Some consider him one of the representative figures in medicine of his time because of his Latin medical works. Scholars have identified seventy-two medical works by him, some of which were translated into Catalan or other languages (*OC*, 2:19–43).[12] For example, *Regimen sanitatis* (Rule of health), written for James II in 1305, was translated into Catalan at the queen's request. Arnau's medical works became better known after the invention of printing, especially in the sixteenth and seventeenth centuries, when numerous editions appeared.

Arnau's medical practices follow in the tradition of Galen and Hippocrates although he supplemented his Greek sources with Arabic and Hebrew works. His commentaries on Galen and his translations from Arabic to Latin of works by Avicenna, Albuzale, and Avenzoar helped him develop a systematic science of medicine. However, his major contribution to medicine was to fuse the Western empirical tradition with Greek and Arab medical philosophy.

Arnau's medical influence continued after his death. His contributions to thirteenth-century medicine, according to George Sydney Brett, parallel those of Roger Bacon in thirteenth-century physics.[13] Also, his attempts to measure the qualitative intensities of compound medicine, although inconclusive, may have provided the stimulus for Bradwardine's Law.[14]

Arnau's beliefs in the theory of spirits represent an intermediate stage between Hippocrates and sixteenth-century scientists such as Paracelsus, whose doctrine of the vital spirit devoid of its magical characteristics influenced Descartes and students of physiology.[15]

Religious Works in Catalan

Despite the destruction of Arnau's Catalan religious works in 1316, four written discourses and two letters were preserved at the Ecclesiastical Archives at Morella, the Royal Archives of Aragon in Barcelona, and the Royal Academy of Spanish History (*OC,* 1:81–84). Although brief, these four works reveal much about Arnau's beliefs and aspirations.

Arnau had defended himself from vehement attacks in a Latin discourse, *Confessio Ilerdensis* (Confession of Lérida), which he mentioned several times in *Confessió de Barcelona* presented at an assembly presided over by James II. In this presentation Arnau became aggressive and impassioned when defending his ideas, a result of his censorship by Sorbonne theologians and his subsequent forced confession of guilt. Also, disillusioned with papal authority, Arnau began to convey his beliefs in the vernacular to his king and civil government, thereby defending ideas against his clerical adversaries. Arnau's discourse at Barcelona is an important defense of his Franciscan Spiritual and apocalyptic beliefs and a defense against attacks on these beliefs (*OC,* 1:138).

Arnau began *Confessió de Barcelona* with a formal invocation to James II, set forth his evangelical goals, and summarized injustices the clergy committed against him. He then introduced a series of emphatic statements, all of which began with the word "confés" ("I confess") and which predicted the Antichrist's advent. Rather than a public confession of guilt, these statements represent a forceful and haughty profession in which Arnau offers eight proofs of Antichrist's coming, borrowed from Joachim of Flora and his disciples, along with several anticlerical digressions. His sources included the Bible (Daniel, Matthew, Paul, the Apocalypse); medieval compendia (*Glossa ordinaria* [Ordinary gloss of Walafrid Estrab]); medieval legends (the visions of Methodius, the martyr; Cyril of Constantinople; Eusebius; and Hildegard) (*OC,* 1:58–62). However, Arnau's overdependence on sources in the section enumerating apocalyptic proofs is the main defect in the discourse. In addition, such an amalgam of sources proved scandalous, according to Martí de Riquer, especially in ecclesiastical circles: "Arnau cited such suspect and apocryphal texts, mingling these with scriptual quotes, a dangerous and alarming combination of deceits and fantasies with revealed truths."[16]

The importance of *Confessió de Barcelona* lies in its being possibly the origin of Arnau's major work, *Expositio super Apocalypsi* (Exposition on the Apocalypse).[17] As a literary work, *Confessió de Barcelona* excels because of Arnau's vigorous defense, the direct and popular language (except for the formalized incipit), and his lively and emotional presentation. His passion at times becomes threatening. Arnau avidly and selfishly clings to his ideas, contradicting the clergy, who regarded him as an intruder in theological circles: "The College of Theology at Paris rejected his interpretation [of the scriptural passages], not because of error or false premise—which they admittedly could not find—but rather because of fear, for they thought it presumptous that a married man might either announce or write that which they have neither taught nor written" (*OC*, 1:111).

Arnau wrote the *Lliçó de Narbona* (Lesson of Narbonne) during Clement V's papacy, a time of increased activity in Beguine communities of southern France and northern Italy. This work, which Arnau presented to Beguines probably in Narbonne, has an historical, social, and religious importance, for it summarizes his religious beliefs and those of late medieval Beguines and Spirituals.

Scholars have not determined the genre of *Lliçó de Narbona* because it is partly a discourse with didactic notes and partly a sermon. Nonetheless, Arnau gave his work qualities different from *Confessió de Barcelona*. Given his heterogeneous audience, Arnau used simple language and a clear style which the unlearned Beguines understood: "each person should neither desire to know the future nor pretend he or another is God, the emperor, or a prince. On the contrary, one should remember that both he and his neighbor are like burros of the Lord, who can send them to the grain mill or make them carry wood, or whatever task he wishes them to do; and all such tasks should be done with happiness and satisfaction, in such a manner that they should pray: 'Lord, I wish that your will be done, not mine' " (*OC*, 1:166).

Arnau also conveyed his message using *exempla*, which, unlike those of Ramon Llull, lack subtlety and organization. To clarify his evangelical message, Arnau sometimes employed similes, on one occasion comparing the grain mill to the human heart, which continually turns in it thoughts and desires: the grain of wheat (Christ), if ground correctly, provides life and nourishment; however, if the Christian desires worldly goods, he grinds millet; if he desires carnal pleasure, he grinds mud and pitch; if he desires evil, he grinds sand (*OC*, 1:156–57).

The placid tone of *Llicó de Narbona* also differs from the acrid defensive attitude of Arnau's first discourse due mainly to the nature and audience of the presentation. The esprit de corps between Arnau and the Beguines required humility for most of his didactic delivery. However, toward the end of his discourse, Arnau launches sarcastic attacks on the clergy and the Scholastic method, attacks which led to the 1316 condemnation of the Latin version, no longer extant, and the Catalan version. Despite this censorship, however, Beguines rapidly circulated the written discourse and had it translated into Italian and modern Greek.

In 1309 Arnau took on several diplomatic missions for James II, Frederick III, and Cardinal Jacopo Colonna, who supported the Spirituals, Beguines, and others. When asked to account for his diplomatic activities, he presented *Interpretatio de visionibus in somniis* before the Avignon papal court. Arnau's Catalan reproduction of this lost discourse, minus the section relating James II's and Frederick III's dreams, is *Raonament d'Avinyó* (Reasoning of Avignon).

Although he repeated former themes (for example, apocalyptic trends, anticlericalism, anti-Scholasticism, equality of humankind, life of poverty), Arnau introduced new preoccupations in *Raonament d'Avinyó:* the qualities of a good ruler, the tyrant, the rich who seek glorification at the expense of the poor, the missionary ideal and military crusade. By incorporating these changes, Arnau emphasized his wish to conquer non-Christians and to identify the kings of Aragon and Sicily as the rulers God chose to combat the Antichrist. Through these slight modifications, Arnau described his new role: "Christ, who in these times made me his trumpeter, now has given me a new role as currier of the king of Aragon and his brother Frederick. All that I have announced to the church of Rome and to other centers of Christianity, the Lord has made me reveal to these two brothers and their people, so that, according to certain signs, He now wishes, in this last century, to put forth the truth of Christianity, specifically through these two brothers and their households, as you are about to hear" (*OC*, 1:168–69).

Raonament d'Avinyó surpasses Arnau's remaining Catalan presentations because he altered its tone to conform to new themes and his new role. According to Jordi Rubió i Balaguer, Arnau begins in a calm, storytelling fashion, builds up to an impassioned attack on the clergy, the wealthy, and evil princes, and ends in a tranquil but persuasive tone.[18]

Arnau's modifications in tone also affect the style of *Raonament d'Avinyó,* which goes from popular to eloquent as he attempts to convince ecclesiastical authority of his plans for a military crusade. Also, its autobiographical nature and, as Menéndez y Pelayo observes, its documentation of customs and language, add to its significance.[19]

In *Informació espiritual* (Spiritual information), which he directed to Frederick III in 1310, Arnau subjected material he discussed in previous treatises to a more rigorous organization. He began with the king's duties to God, insisting that he imitate Christ's life, and summarized the queen's duties and habits, including passages on reading and learning for women that may have influenced Francesc Eiximenis's *Llibre de les dones* (Book for women). Arnau then specified rules for governing and royal obligations toward the common good: tolerance toward other religious groups, help for the poor, and rejection of an ostentatious way of life. He ends by advocating religious universality.

Conclusion

Arnau's prose style lacks the artistic simplicity of Llull's and the rhetorical exuberance of the Catalan humanists, as Miquel Batllori observes: "his prose represents an intermediate stage between that of Llull and the didactic, pre-humanistic style of Francesc Eiximenis" (*OC,* 1:54). The style of *Informació espiritual,* indeed, is later reflected in Eiximenis's treatises, which are characterized by organization, reliance on religious sources, and thematic development. Arnau's thoughts are well organized, clear, and precise, despite frequent digressions.[20] Arnau's sincerity and impulsiveness bring about his spontaneity and modulations in style and tone. Concomitantly, the psychological development and personal information in his works reveal his extroverted personality. Finally, his popular language, democratic ideal, and mundane and picturesque prose reflect his respect for humans and his identification with the common people. A controversial figure given to apocalyptic tendencies, Arnau left behind him a valuable record of moral and social ideas and medical knowledge that are important to our understanding of thirteenth-century Europe.

Chapter Four

The Catalan Chronicles and *The Chronicle of James I*

The Latin Tradition and Catalan Translations

In the late tenth century, the monastery of Ripoll became the center and depository of Catalan culture. Its cultural hegemony lasted until the thirteenth century, when it was replaced by the Cistercian monastery of Poblet. The Benedictines of Ripoll codified the history and religious culture of medieval Catalonia and recorded the accomplishments of the counts of Barcelona. *Gesta comitum barcinonensium* (Deeds of the earldom of Barcelona), their leading work of historiography, includes sections on the Catalan kings added to the original compilation (1162–84). This chronicle therefore covers the history of Catalonia from its origin to 1299 and is the basic historical source on the counts of Barcelona. It appeared in Latin and in Catalan, the latter being a translation of a lost Latin manuscript.

In addition, Jaume Massó Torrents discovered a chronicle written in Catalan and identified it as a translation of *De rebus Hispaniae* (On Hispanic affairs) by Rodrigo de Toledo (Rodrigo Jiménez de Rada, archbishop of Toledo).[1] Pere Ribera de Perpejà had translated this work freely, omitting passages and interpolating episodes (e.g., the treason of Count Ganelon), and had entitled it *Crònica d'Espanya* (Chronicle of Spain, 1268).[2]

The Hypothetical Epic Narrative

In his attentive reading of *Crònica de Jaume I* (*The Chronicle of James I*, 1213–76), Manuel de Montoliu discovered several prose narratives he believed were based on epic poems.[3] Though first opposed by scholars, Montoliu's theory has gradually gained acceptance. Based on rhythm, on assonance in the chronicles of James I, Bernat Desclot, Ramon Muntaner, and on French and Castilian epic poetry and themes, other scholars joined Montoliu in reconstructing hypothetical epic nar-

33

ratives. (Ferran Soldevila, for example, printed over three thousand verses in his edition of the four chronicles.) These scholars applied the theories of oral tradition and studies of Ramón Menéndez Pidal and A̶l̶a̶n̶ Bates Albert Lord to a supposed epic verse tradition in medieval Catalonia, a tradition based on Carolingian epic themes, Arthurian verse romances, and Castilian epics. The French material may have been transformed to Provençal before reaching Catalonia. Also, hypothetical epic poetry or verse romances dealing with Catalan material may have existed and was probably sung and/or written in Provençal or Aragonese. Also, most epic verse narratives in Catalan chronicles, which appear in highly dramatic sections, such as battle scenes, and in dialogue form, are historical epics based on contemporary historical events.

The Chronicle of James I

Authorship and Textual History. Most scholars believe that James I either wrote *Crònica de Jaume I,* also known as *Llibre dels Feyts* (Book of deeds), or supervised its composition by scribes.[4] The first theory was proposed by Ferran Soldevila on the basis of internal evidence: the use of "I" and the royal "we"; the personal nature of certain references; the subjective style and views James held; phrases, such as, "G. de Puyo, who is with me at the time that I am writing this book";[5] the intensity and psychological argumentation of certain passages; and the absence of erudite, classical, and Latin learning and references, excluding the preface, which a clergyman probably wrote later (*QG,* 16–18).

The second supposition, that James directed and intervened in writing his chronicle, has received wider acceptance, for in the Middle Ages a work supervised by a monarch was attributed to him. In their efforts to identify the person, or persons, who committed James's words to paper, scholars have become convinced that *The Chronicle of James I* was written at two intervals and that one person was primarily responsible for the writing during each period.

Bernat Vidal's authorship of the first section is based on two references to him in the chronicle, one of which describes Vidal as a learned man who accompanied James in a military campaign (*CJ,* 1:342).[6] Jaume Sa Roca's authorship of the last section is however more plausible because he not only accompanied James on military expeditions but also later became the bishop of Huesca.[7]

Along with its authorship, scholars have offered several explanations for the textual history of *The Chronicle of James I* and for the reconstruction of its Catalan manuscripts. Lluís Nicolau d'Olwer believed that the events of 1228 to 1240 and those of 1265 to 1276 contain concrete references to names, details, and events. On the other hand, the brief and rapid narration of the years 1242 to 1264 lacks specifics such as names of historic figures, an omission due to James's failure to recall names. Therefore, the writing of the first part (chaps. 2–327) must have taken place in the 1240s, possibly 1244, as indicated by James's mention of G. de Puyo (Guillem I de Puyo), who accompanied the king at Játiva in 1244. A second writing perhaps (chaps. 328–546), which includes events from 1242 to 1276, was begun in 1274 under James's intervention and completed after his death (1276).[8]

Manuscript studies of *The Chronicle of James I* have also produced different theories. Nicolau d'Olwer believed that the original Catalan version, now lost, formed the basis for Pere Marsili's Latin translation of James's chronicle (1313).[9] This translation and the hypothetical 1276 manuscript, or a copy of it, were used to compile the manuscript that forms the basis of the extant Poblet copy (1343). Nicolau d'Olwer assumed that Marsili changed the first-person references to third person and added and modified material, such as the description of winds, didactic passages, and classical citations.[10] Soldevila rejected Nicolau d'Olwer's theory of Marsili's influence on the extant manuscripts pending a detailed comparative analysis of the Latin and Poblet manuscripts (*QG*, 62). However, Nicolau d'Olwer's theory is important because it partially explains several lacunae in existing manuscripts.

Themes and Character. *The Chronicle of James I* may be the first autobiographical chronicle in the vernacular to survive. No doubt the historical tradition emanating from Ripoll motivated its authors. In addition, several motives evidently compelled James to compose his chronicle: to immortalize his reign and lineage, to transmit his good image, and to glorify God for selecting him as king. As a result, James's biography overshadows the historical events in which he does not appear. His dominating figure, the first-person narration, and the careful chronological sequence unify the work.

James may also have envisioned a popular chronicle accessible to his most faithful subjects, the Catalans. The work James and his scribes produced was meticulous, chronological, and usually, but not always, historical. Its poetry in prose gives it an epic tone that is present in both its form and style as Nicolau d'Olwer notes: "One cannot construct meters here; the conventionalisms of the epic phraseology were consecrated over a century before, by a truly international tradition in Western Europe."[11]

A martial atmosphere also pervades a major part of *The Chronicle of James I,* especially the chapters on the conquest of Mallorca and Valencia and on the internal rebellion among the Aragonese nobility. Since James's pride lies in the Mallorcan and Valencian conquests, the authors narrated these victories (chaps. 98–287) in the greatest detail, combining biographical and poetic elements. They relied heavily on epic poetry for battle scenes and events depicting these triumphs, according to Soldevila, who constructed over 1,800 hypothetic epic verses. By fusing biography and poetry in this section, the authors created a pleasant combination of reality and poetry and added an epic tone and character (*QG,* 198–313).

James's preoccupation with casting himself in a politically favorable light caused the authors to omit unpleasant and embarrassing events and decisions of James's reign: the Treaty of Corbeil (Corbell), his unsuccessful attempt to place his son on the throne of Navarre, and the injury to the bishop of Gerona. Clearly James's image and not objectivity became the motive for writing.

Throughout the chronicle God's will and providence guide the fates of James and of his warriors. Before each battle James prays to Christ and Mary and regards his victories as providential. However, he considers man not a pawn of the supernatural but rather a creature of action. The king of Navarre supports this belief, insisting on the king's good deeds: "Well do you know, king, that when the hour of death comes we kings take from this world nothing but a shroud apiece, which is indeed of better cloth than those of other people; but this only remains of us from the great power we once had, that we can serve God with it, and leave behind a good name for the good deeds we did. If in this world we do not do them, there will come no other time in which we can" (*CJ,* 1:246).

The balance between providence and human will and action is most important, according to Arthur Terry: "there is a strong sense of the workings of Providence and of the value which lies in recording individual feats of heroism. Both themes are handled with a notable lack of exaggeration: if God appears to favour the Catalans, there are no spectacular interventions of the supernatural, and the bravery of the Catalan troops is set firmly in a background of detailed strategies."[12] Also, James humbly accepts two miraculous occurrences related in the chronicle, both of which have a tangential importance. As a result, by emphasizing his good deeds, the authors fulfill both James's didactic motives and his desire to immortalize his accomplishments.[13]

The Chronicle of James I represents more than a series of strategic maneuvres and military expeditions. For example, the authors use superlatives when they speak of patriotism, an essential ideal, in order to convey feelings and emotions when describing the lands James rules and his respect for the laws of each political division.[14] However, James felt a special affinity toward Catalans, especially the supportive city dwellers whom he praised at the expense of the Aragonese (*CJ*, 2:514). He advises his son-in-law, Alphonse X of Castile—depicted as a slightly weak, irresolute, though sincere king—to respect two alliances: "the church, and the people and cities of the country" (*CJ*, 2:617).

The chroniclers depict James as more than a military strategist and ruler of high ideals. He shows emotion and suffers human feelings: anger, suffering, sorrow, tears, and insomnia. However, the frequent scenes of his weeping for soldiers killed in battle are meant not to reveal weakness but to show his humanity, sense of duty, and tribute to the dead (*QG*, 23–24). Also, he is merciful to the Islamic enemy. In order to further his aims, James becomes cunning and devious, capable of transgressions against his creator and of deceit and bribery. Proud and resolute, James always acts decisively and conceals his political blunders; obsessed with justice, he often punishes his soldiers with death. His pride, obstinacy, and exaggerated sense of justice, however, represent good and necessary qualities in a king, and make James superior to his irresolute and weak peers Sancho of Navarre, Alphonse X, and the Saracen chiefs. James therefore becomes the hero of the chronicle, but in doing so retains his humanness.

Language, Style, and Sources.   Scholars have attempted to fix the date of the oldest extant manuscript by studying its archaic language. In a study on morphological, phonetic, and lexical details common to other chronicles, Montoliu concluded that *The Chronicle of James I* was written in the late thirteenth century.[15] Soldevila questioned this date when he found that the semantic and syntactical particularities are rare even in thirteenth-centry prose (*QG*, 29–33).

In addition to its language, the style of *The Chronicle of James I* is noteworthy because of its variety. In dialogue James modulates his speech to correspond to the social class of his interlocutors and the social setting of the event in which he takes part. For example, when confronted with taking several castles and leaving Valencia to the Moors,

James responds to Fernando Diez: "I have arrived at the time and a point at which I can take Valencia, and so I intend having the hen and the chickens too" (*CJ*, 1:357). This use of proverbs and adages gives a colloquial air to the king's speech; also, dialogue, often in the form of short sentences and phrases, produces a rapid, direct, and realistic effect.

Except for the erudite preface, the style of the chronicle is unaffected and spontaneous; however, at times lacunae and carelessness obfuscate several difficult passages. In addition, other stylistic problems exist: improper use of verbal tense and mood; reduced syntactical constructions; erroneous subject and verb concordance; a lack of erudite words and polished prose structures. This style reveals James's colloquial style, a reflection of the spoken language, and indicates that James dictated extensively to scribes who transcribed the work.

James's chroniclers create a technique that reappeared in the Catalan fifteenth-century novel: they maintain the action throughout and omit dry, meticulous, or explanatory digressions. More specifically, they hold the reader's attention by using changing scenarios, animated dialogue, brief but pointed descriptions and explanations, and a constant flow of characters. Into the action and dialogue they intertwine epic and lyric poetry, such as the maritime passages surrounding the conquest of Mallorca: "and it made a fine sight for those who stayed on land and for us, for all the sea seemed white with sails, so large a fleet was it" (*CJ*, 1:113); "early on the third day, between sunrise and tierce, we were at Portopi, my flag was hoised on each of the galleys, and at the sound of trumpets we entered the city of Mallorca" (*CJ*, 1:210). Finally, to convey a greater sense of reality, they narrate in the first person singular or in the plural form "nós" (we), a common form for royal documents.

On the surface the authors seem to use dialogue to create greater verisimilitude. For instance, the master of the Order of the Temple uses French words in his speech, while the subjects of Montpellier utter Provençal expressions; the pope speaks short phrases in Latin and Italian, while nobles and kings of central Spain speak Castilian and Aragonese; Saracens introduce Arabic words in their Romance speech.[16] A closer look at these passages reveals that authors simply introduce foreign words, phrases, and passages as a literary convention, disregarding the basic colloquial patterns of the non-Catalan languages. As Antoni Badia i Margarit concludes, "inserting fragments in other languages was both

capricious and incongruent."[17] He therefore rules out the authors' desire
for verisimilitude.

Scholars find it difficult to identify the sources of *The Chronicle of
James I* because this work is autobiographical and contains hypothetical
epic verse. French epics such as *Chançon de Guillaume* (Song of Guillaume), *Chevalerie Vivien* (Knighthood of Vivien) and the Spanish
Poema del Mío Cid (*Poem of the Cid*) may have inspired its epic quality.[18]
Also, allusions to biblical passages indicate that the Bible influenced its
content. And based on its solid historical foundation and chronological
precision, the authors probably consulted royal documents when writing
the chronicle.[19]

The Chronicle of James I differs substantially from thirteenth-century
narratives and poems in which the king or knight becomes an ideal
model of chivalry. By emphasizing James's human nature and the
autobiographical character and colloquial style of the chronicle, the
authors created a unique work in its time. Though scholars have
unsuccessfully sought to identify previous models of James's work, they
have found only faint resemblances to fragmentary Latin narratives. In
general, however, *The Chronicle of James I* follows the tradition of
Augustine's *Confessions*.[20]

Summary and Conclusion

This first of four great Catalan chronicles is an innovative work of
its genre because of its epic tone, and simple, popular language and
style. Given the universal nature of Ramon Llull's works, *The Chronicle
of James I* can be considered the first manifestation of the Catalan spirit
in Catalan prose. Patriotism and a feeling for the land and kingdom
distinguish it from chronicles that simply recount the history of an
epoch. By focusing the action upon the deeds and convictions of the
first-person narrator, the authors succeed in presenting a particular and
often subjective interpretation of history through the psyche of one of
the leading Catalan monarchs.

Narrative art and a subjective technique make *The Chronicle of James
I* a precursor of leading narrative prose of fifteenth-century and Renaissance Catalonia. The authors strive for verisimilitude through an agile
and popular prose, animated dialogues, proverbs, adages, humor, and
intimate details and quotidian allusions that contrast with the lofty
nature of the king's enterprises.

On the other hand, the chronicle contains lacunae—defects the scribes may have caused—and an uneven character of detail and description in the different sections. Scholars attribute the latter problem to the sequential writing on at least two hypothetical dates (1244, 1274), therefore making it difficult to recall events that occurred between 1242 and 1265. Despite these problems, *The Chronicle of James I* stands as a historic monument of epic dimension.

Chapter Five
Bernat Desclot's *Chronicle*
Authorship, Title, and Date

The second major Catalan chronicle was probably written by a prominent person, for its content, style, and personal references suggest an author attached to the royal chancellery. Since the name Bernat Desclot, which appears in the incipit, cannot be found in royal documents, Desclot must be a pseudonym.

Research has yielded two possible authors, who share similar backgrounds: Jaspert de Botonac and Bernat Escrivà.[1] The former became the bishop of Valencia (1276), played a major role in the final scene of the chronicle, and was perhaps the brother of Pere Arnau de Botonac, who witnessed several major episodes narrated in the chronicle. The latter formed part of the chancelleries of James I and Peter II, who named him treasurer. Further, his ancestors had come from the town of Es Clot; given the informal use of surnames in the Middle Ages, he could have easily taken the surname Desclot (d'Es Clot) from Es Clot and identified himself in the chronicle as Bernat Desclot (*QG*, 56).[2] Finally, the dependence on legal documents suggests that a member of the royal chancellery could have authored the work.

Due to deviations in the incipit, the title of the chronicle is uncertain. Although the manuscript at the National Library of Spain refers to Desclot's chronicle as the "Book of King Peter of Aragon and his Predecessors," other manuscripts bear the title "Noble Kings of Aragon, who Were of High Lineage and of the Noble Count of Barcelona,"[3] an acceptable title because Desclot dedicated the first fifty chapters to Catalan-Aragonese unity and to the reigns of Ramon Berenguer IV, Alphonse I, Peter I, and James I of Catalonia. The remaining chapters, which deal with Peter the Great's reign, take up over two thirds of the chronicle, a fact which led F. L. Critchlow to entitle his translation *Chronicle of the Reign of King Pedro III of Aragon*.[4] However, scholars prefer the title "Chronicle of Desclot" for its brevity and exactitude.

Desclot began the chronicle in April 1283, a date that indicates that the conquest of Sicily inspired his work. He probably interrupted his

41

writing in 1285, when the French army laid siege to Gerona, and finished it between 1286 and 1288 or certainly before 20 June 1295.[5]

Divisions, Contrasts with *The Chronicle of James I,* Characters, and Characteristics

The initial fifty chapters vary significantly in length, lack chronological order, and are based primarily on legendary and epic sources. Conversely, the remaining chapters (51–168), are proportionate, coherent, unified, and founded mostly on documents and eyewitness reports. Desclot's chronicle contrasts with *The Chronicle of James I.* In characterizing Peter, Desclot strove for objectivity, a tendency that stands in contrast to the heroic description of James in *The Chronicle of James I.* Also, unlike the author of *The Chronicle of James I,* Desclot made his king, and not Catalonia or the House of Aragon, the object of his patriotism.[6] Whereas the author of *The Chronicle of James I* described James as an astute military and political strategist and a virile warrior, Desclot concentrated on the psychological development of Peter, stressing his evolution from a rash youth to a serene monarch and finally to a benign, somewhat repentant aging man. Desclot conceded that Peter had to assert himself to subdue his opponents but praised his loyalty to and respect for his father and affirmed his humility during the French invasion when misfortune convinced him that he was his creator's servant.

Desclot also emphasized Peter's virtues by comparing him to the malicious French. According to Desclot, Peter succeeded because of "his stoutness of heart . . . and the help from God" (*CR,* 2:234); however, the cowardly French, whose arrogance led them to trust in their power and numbers, desecrated churches and brutally murdered and raped women in Roussillon. Desclot also contrasted Peter with his French counterparts, Charles of Anjou and Philip III: Peter mourned his dead while Charles and Philip reacted angrily and bitterly to military defeat (*CR,* 2:116). Furthermore, Desclot's antipathy toward the French and devotion to Peter led him to describe Philip as a coward, whose pomp contrasted with Peter's simplicity and manliness.

Despite his admiration, Desclot idealized Peter less than other chroniclers did their protagonists. He described the adult Peter as "sore, distraught and perplexed with doubt" (*CR,* 2:84), "overcome with drowsiness" (*CR,* 2:119). High nobles reprimanded the king for giving "no heed soever to this warfare against the King of France" (*CR,*

2:305). On the other hand, Peter occasionally compensated for his weaknesses by merciless actions: to provide an example he drowned three hundred enemy troops and tore out the eyes of another 260 before binding them and sending them back to the French king (*CR*, 2:352); he dealt with revolt by having Ferran Sanxis drowned (*CR*, 1:206); and he punished disobedience by executing his soldiers who murdered the Jews of Gerona and pillaged their quarter (*CR*, 2:285).

Desclot praised the heroism and loyalty of Peter's soldiers, such as Viscount Ramon Folch, whose small army defended Gerona in the king's absence. His role took on epic proportions when he refused to let the count of Foix persuade him to join forces with Philip III against Peter. Desclot also heralded Roger de Llúria's naval conquests and emotional discourses.

Wishing to remain a passive observer or perhaps a hidden omniscient author, Desclot introduced several chapters with the formulaic phrase: "the story now goes on to tell" or "and now the book ceases to speak of . . . and will begin to tell" (*CR*, 2:vi). Although he witnessed some events he described (*CR*, 2:327), Desclot did not wish to become a character in his chronicle, perhaps to ensure its objectivity.

Desclot's greatest merit, his historicity, surfaces especially in chapters on Peter's reign, in which he relied on legal documents, royal dispatches, and treatises.[7] He wrote on unpleasant topics, such as the suzerain with the feudal nobles of Aragon, a subject that Ramon Muntaner, who also wrote a chronicle on Peter II, preferred to avoid. As a result of his anonymity, dependence on documents, and preoccupation with historical accounts, Desclot became for historians a reliable source and a "model chronicler of the Middle Ages."[8]

The First Fifty Chapters

The first fifty chapters of the chronicle are diverse because Desclot wished to include all pertinent information on the Catalan-Aragonese kingdom from its inception following the battle of Fraga (1134). He chose this method perhaps to provide background material for the chapters on Peter. The years separating him from the origins of the Catalan-Aragonese union and his preoccupation with legitimacy, especially that of James I, led him to rely on legends and oral epic poetry. As a result, these chapters become chivalric and at times fantastic.

The epic tone, hypothetical verse narratives, and references to Roland, Alexander, and other figures confirm that Desclot no doubt knew the chivalric and epic literature filtering into Catalonia from the north. Desclot, however, modified legends that may have been based on epic poems. For example, he fused the historic accounts of two persons with the same name, Guillem Ramon de Montcada, into one legend.[9] In addition, he relied on preexistent epic verse in the first three chapters and in chapter 4, the legendary account of James's conception,[10] basing it on Arthurian and Carolingian sources and on Geoffrey of Monmouth's *Histories of the Kings of Britain*.[11] In addition, he used episodes from epic verse on the conquests of Ubeda, Muret, Mallorca, and Murcia. He relied so heavily on French and Provençal epic models that, except for Peter II, his characters become more literary than real.[12]

The most perfect and lyrical legendary account, that of the Good Count of Barcelona and the empress of Germany, is the longest of the four legends in Desclot's chronicle (chaps. 7–10). Based upon the legends of Gundeberga and of Bernard of Septimania and Judith, this account spread throughout Western Europe and entered Catalonia via Provence, where a troubadour disseminated it. Unconstrained by historical veracity, Desclot created an imaginary episode about how Provence became part of the domain of the count of Barcelona. By emphasizing the humility of the count, who withheld his identity from everyone but the empress, Desclot created suspense and built his narration to a climax.

Desclot also combined several episodes from his sources to stress the count's valor and determination. For example, when the count realizes that the knight of Provence is absent, he himself must defend her against both prosecuting knights. After he roundly defeats the first accuser, the remaining knight admits guilt and his intention to defame the empress, an admission that removes all suspicion of her unfaithfulness. To show the count's modesty and noble breeding, Desclot added an epilogue in which the count steals away at night and begins his return to Barcelona, initially declining a handsome reward from the emperor until the empress recalls him to receive the land of Provence.

Chapters on Peter the Great

In the chapters on the French invasion of Catalonia, Desclot maintained a chronological development in the scenes he narrated: the French camp, the resistance in Catalonia, Roger de Llúria's naval maneuvers, Peter's expeditions through Catalonia. By using political and moral counsel and reflections, maxims, proverbs, and popular adages, Desclot made these chapters didactic, a quality missing in the initial part of his chronicle.

He also used proverbs to abbreviate long moral lessons. At times he based his moral-didactic passages on the Bible, such as the following example from Matthew 10:36: "the sage hath said in an ancient proverb that there is no foe so strong as he that is of one's own household, so therefore if such an [*sic*] one be a subject of the realm, he can work more harm than may appear" (*CR*, 2:193).

Desclot's prose contains two distinguishing characteristics: attention to detail and preference for description. His numerous details on courtly and martial life suggest that he was a professional writer attached to the Catalan court.[13] His precise descriptions, such as that of the Almogavers, foot soldiers who fought for the Catalan kings, convey an accurate historic picture (*CR*, 2:28–29). At times his obsession with detail and his lengthy discussion of political intrigue, battle preparations, military strategy, and legal matters detract from the action and try the reader's patience.

Desclot's talent for creating dramatic action is evident in two scenes involving Almogavers, one of whom left the galley to defend his friend in peril (*CR*, 2:98–99), and the other who defeated a French knight before the French prince (*CR*, 2:103–5). In addition, Peter's compassion for the suffering masses after the defeat of Peralada (*CR*, 2:278–79) and his sorrow for his dying father (*CR*, 2:4) indicate his mastery of evoking pathos.

Style and Language

Desclot created some of the best dialogues in medieval Catalan literature by using natural, logical, and animated verbal exchanges and popular expressions to sway his reader's sentiments and to explain pertinent facts. His leading dialogues include Peter's words with the messenger during the seige of Messina (*CR*, 2:76–77) and his conversation with the seneschal John de Greilly, who revealed that King Charles wanted to make a mockery of the duel of Bordeaux and deceitfully seize Peter (*CR*, 2:113–14). Peter can be sarcastic as his feined humility and polite words to the rebel Berenger Oller suggest (*CR*, 2:192). He also can be comical and ironic as he was when the chamberlain dared not wake James, Peter's brother and ruler of Mallorca: "Can it be indeed that a man is able to sleep thus soundly!" (*CR*, 2:204). In answer to Peter's question on the construction of James of Mallorca's castle, the master workman replies: "Methinks not even a rat could creep away unseen, so strict a watch hath the King of Aragon set upon this castile" (*CR*, 2:205). Roger de Llúria proudly answers the count of Foix concerning his naval power: "I verily believe that not only a galley or a ship of burthen could sail the seas but that not even a fish would dare rise out therefrom unless it should bear the device or arms of the King of Aragon upon its tail" (*CR*, 2:354).

Desclot reproduced brief and clear speeches, especially discourses with the counselors of the king of France on the invasion into Catalonia. Among the most dramatic speeches is that of the French papal legate Cholet, who took part in the French expedition against Catalonia (*CR*, 2:xiv, 217–19).

Besides its dependence on epic phraseology and formulas, Desclot's prose has an internal coherence which he achieved in part by repeating words, such as the connector "e" (and) and "puis" (well, so), by using stylistic patterns, such as parallelism, and by developing well-organized and focused paragraphs.[14]

The manuscripts of Desclot's chronicle are among the oldest of the four Catalan chronicles, especially manuscript 486 (Library of Catalonia), which dates from the end of the thirteenth century, that is, before the 1344 manuscript of *The Chronicle of James I*. It is therefore rich in archaic and dialectical forms that characterize individuals from northeast Catalonia.[15] Although in the chronicle Peter's adversaries speak French, his French sympathizers speak in Catalan. In addition, Desclot's precise use of Arabic names and his positive attitude toward Moors indicate familiarity with Islamic culture and Arabic.

Sources and Influence

Differences in the two sections of the chronicle may have been affected by Desclot's diverse sources, such as epic and legends in part 1 and documents and eyewitness accounts in part 2. Although he relied much on epic material for part 1, he also used documents and other chronicles for the initial fifty chapters. These include the chronicle of Rodrigo Jiménez de Rada, French and Provençal historical sources, the traditions of Valencian Moors, and documents[16]—though he questioned the content of *The Chronicle of James I* for James's conquest of Saracen lands. In chapters on Peter the Great's reign, he consulted documentary evidence including a letter the king sent rebellious barons. In the chapter on the Angevin challenge of Bordeaux, he supplied a verbatim rendition of the agreement. And in chapter 139, he quoted a vernacular version of a Catalan statute (*usatge*), a further indication of his legal interest.

The number of fourteenth-century manuscripts and its influence on *Curial i Güelfa* attest to the popularity of Desclot's chronicle. Historians of past centuries consulted and partially reproduced the chronicle because of its historicity. Also, Desclot's work was admired and used by Pedro Antonio Beuter and by Jerónimo Zurita, who wrote *Segunda parte de la crónica general de toda España* (Second part of the general chronicle of Spain, 1551) and *Anales de la Corona de Aragón* (Annals of the crown of Aragon, 1562), respectively. In the nineteenth century Alexandre Buchon edited the chronicle and Michele Amari quoted it in his study of the Sicilian vespers.[17] Louis-Charles Romey inserted passages verbatim from Desclot into *Histoire d'Espagne* (1838–51). In addition, Rafael Cervera's Spanish translation was partially reproduced in the late eighteenth century, especially the portions on the French invasion, which served to enkindle patriotic fervor among Spaniards in the midst of the French invasion (1793). The chronicle was also translated into Italian and selected passages translated into Aragonese.

Evaluation and Conclusion

Desclot's chronicle differs from the three other major Catalan chronicles because of its historical perspective and its detached third-person author, characteristics that at times make the work impersonal and austere. Nonetheless, his chronicle represents an advance in Catalan prose development, particularly in his use of dialogue and character delineation of Peter the Great. Stylistically, Desclot avoided the pitfalls of hyperbole, digressions, and excessive enumeration; on the contrary, he bound together the internal fabric of his prose with brief, concise, and logical language and a coherent sentence structure.

The obvious deficiency is the external structure. The disparate narration on Count Ramon Berenguer and each king of Aragon leads to the conclusion that Desclot lacked a well-planned scheme for his initial chapters, a flaw evident in the excessive attention he gave to James's Valencian conquest. Although less intense and vigorous than Muntaner and the author of *The Chronicle of James I*, Desclot excelled in his power to observe and the fluency and cohesion of his prose. These qualities, the well-balanced narratives (for example, the Sicilian campaign), and the desire for historical truth have given Desclot the reputation of being an ideal chronicler of the Middle Ages.

Chapter Six
The Chronicle of Muntaner

Biography

The best source for Ramon Muntaner's biography is his *Crònica (The Chronicle of Muntaner)*, his only surviving literary work. Muntaner was born in Peralada (1265) into an affluent burgher family that hosted James I of Aragon, Alphonse X of Castile, and his wife when these figures traveled north. At age ten Muntaner left Peralada (*CM*, 1:2).[1]

In 1301 Muntaner took part in the siege of Messina and remained in southern Italy until joining the Grand Company, a military force made up of Catalans, Aragonese, and mercenaries. He served Roger de Flor, leader of the Company, as procurator general and in other administrative capacities in Sicily, Greece, and Asia Minor. After Roger's death Muntaner governed the important commercial city of Gallipoli until 1307, served Ferdinand of Mallorca from 1307 until 1309, and returned to Messina. While in Messina Frederick of Sicily commissioned him to govern Jerba, which he did until 1315, when he directed a voyage of the future James III of Mallorca from Catania to Perpignan. In 1316 Muntaner was appointed procurator general to Bernat de Sarrià in Valencia, and he later became a *jurat* or counselor of Valencia, a position he held when he attended Alphonse III's coronation at Saragossa in 1328. This king later appointed Muntaner personal counselor to James III of Mallorca and mayor of Ibiza, where he lived until his death in 1336.

General Character and Themes

The most literary of the four chronicles, *The Chronicle of Muntaner* encompasses the years from the birth of James I to the coronation of Alphonse III. However, its action centers around its two major narratives: the French invasion of Catalonia (1285) and the Grand Company's conquests in Greece and Asia Minor (1303–9). The latter campaign, together with the success of the Catalans on the islands and mainland of southern and eastern Italy, gives Muntaner's work the distinction of being not only the chronicle of Catalan-Aragonese expansion but also the only European source of information on the expansion.[2]

Throughout the prologue and first chapter the author glorifies God and the House of Aragon. Muntaner insisted that God favors the Catalan kings, who, despite their condemnation by the pope, remained faithful to Christian beliefs and promoted the conquest of infidels. However, his attitude toward Pope Martin IV is ambiguous; while he accepted papal authority, he secretly disapproved of Martin's preference for Charles I of Anjou and the French. At one point he even blamed the pope's French origins for his approval of a crusade and for the excommunication of Peter II but conceded, "no sentence has ever issued from the court of Rome that is not just; and so we must all believe . . . and so do I believe" (*CM*, 1:179). This statement of belief notwithstanding, Muntaner justified Catalan martial resistance, convinced that in political affairs God's power and will supersede the decisions of Rome. He therefore presented the Catalans as instruments of the Lord.

Throughout the chronicle Muntaner described each member of the Catalan royal family in ideal and superlative terms, extending his hyperbolic descriptions to nobles such as Manfred of Sicily who marry into Catalan royalty: "And the said King Manfred lived more magnificently than any other lord in the world, and with greater doings, and with greater expenditure; so that this marriage pleased the Lord King En Jaime of Aragon and the Lord Infante En Pedro, his son, more than any other in the world. . . . and with ten well-equipped galleys they brought away the damsel, who was fourteen years old and the most beautiful creature and most discreet and virtuous that lived at that time" (*CM*, 1:30).

Muntaner knew that his medieval audience esteemed virtue, especially justice, truth, and mercy, in the Catalan royal family. Therefore, he had to present the members of the House of Aragon as "models of valor and power,"[3] despite the historical reality of a disintegrating empire. Muntaner described the problems threatening the Catalan-Aragonese empire in didactic passages like the following:

And if anyone asks me: "En Muntaner, what proverb is that of the rushes?" it means this: if you tie all the rushes tightly with a rope and want to tear them out all together, I tell you that ten men, however well they pull, cannot tear them out in any way they may try; but if you take off the rope, a boy of eight can pull out the bush, rush by rush, so that not one remains. And so it would be with those three kings [of Catalonia-Aragon, Mallorca and Sicily]; if there were any differences or discord between them (which God forbid) you can reckon upon it that they have such neighbors that they will destroy first one and then the other. (*CM*, 2:710–11)

In his didactic passages, Muntaner offered counsel on political and military concerns. On military strategy, Muntaner wrote the "Sermó" (sermon), tactical advice and admonitions, to Alphonse III on the conquest of Sardinia (*CM*, 2:652–59).[4]

Muntaner preferred Provençal for his poetry but Catalan for his prose. He found unity in the spoken language and expressed it in the following way: "you will find . . . that of people of the same language there are none so numerous as the Catalans. If you speak of Castilians, the true Castile is of small extent and importance; for Castile has many provinces, each with its own language, as different from each other as Catalan and Aragonese. For though Catalans and Aragonese are under one lord, their languages are different. And so likewise will you find it in France and in England and in Germany and in all Romania" (*CM*, 1:73). The first part of this statement is basically correct because of recent Catalan conquests and expansion followed by repopulation with Catalans. Therefore, in Mallorca and Valencia, "sufficient time had not transpired to allow for dialectic variations."[5]

Along with their language he praised Barcelona "the noblest city and finest that the Lord King of Aragon has" (*CM*, 1:60) and described the Catalans of Mallorca as "the most prosperous and well-nurtured people of any city in the world" (*CM*, 1:22). The soldiers of James I provided Muntaner with a motive for another encomium: "the Catalans and Aragonese and all the subjects of the said Lord King of Aragon have more at heart than any other people in the world, for they are full of true love for their sovereigns" (*CM*, 1:40).

The Chronicle of Muntaner as a Literary Creation

An old man dressed in white appeared to Muntaner in a dream, a common device in classical Latin and medieval literatures, to inspire his writing. This mysterious apparition, who insisted that Muntaner write a chronicle, appeared a second time to coax the negligent Muntaner to begin writing.

By selecting this device, Muntaner gave it importance and credibility for his medieval reader[6] and implied that he intended to write a literary rather than historical work. Also, he referred to his work as a "llibre" (book) throughout, never as a chronicle. The use of "llibre" to describe his work led scholars to speculate on its genre; they examined its historical veracity and found that, in addition to creating hyperbolic descriptions of Catalan royalty, Muntaner also distorted statistics; Catalan troops, for example, often go into battle greatly outnumbered and emerge victorious with few casualties. More specifically, he created the impression of a kingdom chosen by God to perform great deeds for his honor. Therefore, rather than a documented account of Catalan expansion, the chronicle becomes royal propaganda emphasizing Catalan-Aragonese unity.

Desiring its acceptance in future generations, Muntaner excluded material such as prejudicial remarks that might blemish the royal family's character and unpleasant situations, including the internal conflicts between king and nobles. The most obvious omissions pertain to the reigns of Peter II and James II, for example, Peter's cruelty toward French prisoners; his fraternal problems with James II of Mallorca; the animosity between Peter II and his father James I; and the opposition between James II and his brother Frederick of Sicily. Although such omissions undermine his historical veracity, Muntaner was more conscious of the didactic content of his work, often preferring "to write a sermon" rather than "to write history." Also, by stressing the didactic function he avoided anecdotes that might place his superiors in a negative light.[7]

However, the chronicle is not a fictitious account completely devoid of a historical basis, for Muntaner recorded his personal experiences and those of eyewitnesses in chronological order even though his propagandist and literary intentions took precedence to historical veracity.

Of all the medieval Catalan chroniclers, Muntaner is the most accomplished writer. His work represents an advanced development in medieval narrative prose and in the Catalan novel largely through several techniques—dramatization, attention to detail, and rhetorical devices.

Among his talents, Muntaner showed skill in creating suspense and building dramatic moments. He carefully developed Charles's plan to battle Peter's troops in an organized one-to-one combat, thus avoiding a revolt in Italy; but before doing so, he penetrated the mind of the cunning French ruler: "When others were sleeping, he was watching, and thought out the wisest plan that any king or other man could even imagine for the restoration of his country and himself" (*CM,* 1:159). In addition, his talent for building climaxes is especially evident when he describes Roger de Flor's activities in Greece and Asia Minor;

the vengeance of the Almogavers at the admiral's death; the battle preparation and attack on Gallipoli; the treason of Berenguer d'Entença wrought by the Genovese and his death at the hands of Bernat de Rocafort's soldiers; the death of the Turkish warrior attempting to escape with his wife from three Catalans; the joust at Calatayud.

Muntaner's preoccupation with detail becomes more pronounced in his description of ceremonies or celebrations involving the House of Aragon, especially the meticulous account of Alphonse's coronation. He particularly used hyperbolical description for regal, festive scenes, and possessions, such as Alphonse's crown.

Throughout the chronicle Muntaner used certain rhetorical devices or formulas, such as "Què us diré"? (What shall I tell you?) and its variants, which have their origin in troubadour expressions and give the author closer rapport with his audience.[8] At times the author anticipated the reader's questions, showing his awareness of his audience: "And if you say: 'En Muntaner, what are those sins you are speaking of?' I could tell you there was pride and arrogance" (CM, 1:697–98). He used interrogative formulas to introduce a new topic, summarize lengthy material, or avoid an issue. Muntaner also preferred these formulas perhaps because he intended his work to be read to an audience, given the widespread illiteracy in the Middle Ages, the nature of his work, and the few manuscripts available.[9] This hypothesis conforms with Muntaner's apologetic and propagandist motives and the popular language of his prose.

Language and Style

The language of *The Chronicle of Muntaner* typifies Catalan literary usage in Muntaner's time. He repeated pronouns, adjectives, such as "alegre" (happy) and the hyperbolic "gran" (great), and adverbs, such as "molt" (very), and "més" (most). He also used colloquial speech, often in hyperbolic statements, and dialectic forms from his native Ampurias (for example, the negation "poc"). In addition, he placed French words in the speech of Charles of Anjou and Philip III of France, and Arab expressions in the speech of Islamic rulers and warriors, thus following a practice established in *The Chronicle of James I.*

Unlike the authors of *The Chronicle of James I,* whose narrative development was linear, Muntaner preferred a shifting narrative, often describing in the same chapter events which take place in different areas of the Mediterranean. For example, in the short chapter 187, he interrupted the action to go on to another happening: "And so I must let the Lord Infante En Pedro be, who holds besieged the city of Leon . . . and must turn again to speak to you of the Lord King of Aragon who is invading the Kingdom of Murcia and enters it by land and by sea" (*CM*, 2:450). This device is common in novels of chivalry, a genre that caters to the actions of different protagonists and is parodied in *Don Quixote de la Mancha*, 1:9.

Of the four major Catalan chronicles, the content of Muntaner's work most resembles the subject matter of Desclot's chronicle since both center on Peter II. However, the style and literary tendencies of both authors differ: Muntaner's writing is personal, hyperbolic, and impassioned, while Desclot's is impersonal, precise, and modest. Muntaner, the soldier-author, dramatized events much more than did Desclot, who preferred objectivity. Furthermore, Muntaner's style and language appear more agile and spontaneous because, unlike Desclot, he felt no need to constantly prove facts. Although both authors wrote didactic works, Muntaner was not preoccupied with teaching morals as was Desclot, whose passages retain an almost sermonlike character. Muntaner's chronicle has more unity for it begins with the birth of James I and ends with Alphonse's coronation (1208–1328); however, Desclot chose to start with the events leading to Catalan-Aragonese unity and continued until Peter II's death (1134–1285). In short, Muntaner's chronicle represents a more advanced development in chronicle writing.

Muntaner's chronicle, according to Josep Miquel Sobré, is a mixture of epic formulas and colloquial expressions that receive new life in his work and reveal information on his character and learning.[10] The colloquial forms go beyond lexical and syntactical uses and include many refrains and proverbs commonly used during Muntaner's time. He knew well the epic and chivalric tradition of England and France, and Provençal verse, but the indigenous Catalan element, especially that of Ampurias, remained with him, affecting his language, style, and perception of reality.

Muntaner's Sources and Influence

Apart from his personal experiences and eyewitness accounts by soldiers who participated in the narrated events, the author drew upon several sources: the Bible and epic and chivalric material of the Carolingian and Breton cycles. Muntaner often employed biblical sources. For example, he compared Peter II, who delivered the Sicilians from the

French, to Moses; he had Roger de Flor's soldiers await him as Jews await the Messiah; he likened the sea voyage of Queen Constanza and princes James and Frederick to Palermo to the Epiphany; and he paralleled the life of Christ and the deeds of Catalan monarchs.

Muntaner's familiarity with epics and romances becomes patent in the epic linguistic formulas of his chronicle as well as in parallels between Catalan kings and their troops and medieval epic heroes. He compared Peter II, "a perfect man" (*CM,,* 1:42), to King Arthur and twice to Alexander, a comparison Desclot also made. The deeds of Peter are superior to those of the Knights of the Round Table (*CM,* 1:340–41). The tournament at Figueras becomes "the finest feats of arms done that had ever been done in a tournament since the time of King Arthur" (*CM,* 2:398).[11]

In addition to biblical and epic sources, Muntaner also used medieval legends of classical themes (Helen and Paris), and personal documents, such as notebooks used to account for supplies. He may also have consulted Desclot's chronicle (*CM,* 1:xxvi; 1:31).[12]

The popularity and importance of the *Chronicle of Muntaner* is evident from its sequel, composed by Admiral Galceran Marquet, and from the various translations of the chronicle: French (1827), German (1842), Italian (1844), Spanish (1860), and English (1920–21). In addition, Muntaner's account of Catalan-Aragonese conquests in Asia Minor and the tragedy of Roger de Flor took on mythical proportions, especially in Spain, in Francisco de Moncada's historical *Expedición de los catalanes y aragoneses contra los turcos y griegos* (*The Catalan Chronicle of Francisco de Moncada,* 1623)[13] and in two nineteenth-century Spanish literary works, Antonio García Gutierrez's *Venganza catalana* (Catalan vengeance) and Vicente Blasco Ibánez's *Los almogávares de Bizancio* (The Almogavers of Byzantium). In no work, however, was Muntaner's influence felt more than in *Tirant lo Blanc,* whose author was inspired by numerous passages of the chronicle. Roger de Flor became one of the models for Tirant, and Muntaner's idealization of narrative history affected Martorell's realistic conception of the novel of chivalry.[14]

Evaluation and Conclusion

Although Muntaner repeated motifs and conventions of previous chroniclers, his spontaneity and the literary qualities of his work made it the most popular of the Catalan chronicles. He intended to write an informative work that would not be entirely dependent on documentation but would exalt the Catalan royal family as model rulers for future generations. In doing so he wrote enthusiastically, describing events he and others had witnessed, especially the Grand Company's activities in Greece and Asia Minor.

According to Eugene Baret, Muntaner's personal approach to the chronicle was novel in the Iberian Peninsula during this time, and perhaps in all of Europe: "In this epoch, I do not see anyone as capable of writing in the historical genre with such a degree of penetration and insight."[15] Perhaps Muntaner can be compared only to Jean de Joinville (1224–1317), who also wrote memoirs in a historical context. But in his own right, Muntaner's skill in building climaxes, dramatizing situations, and animating plots contributed to his chronicle, making it one of the outstanding works of Catalan prose.

Chapter Seven
The *Chronicle* of Peter III

Catalan Culture and Historiography During the Reign of Peter III

Peter III's cultural achievements and promotion of learning parallel those of Alphonse the Wise, whose *Siete Partidas* (Seven divisions of law) Peter ordered translated into Catalan. Like Alphonse, he propagated literature, religion, and science by supporting learned men.[1] An avid correspondent whose letters are among the leading examples of Catalan prose, he also earned the reputation of a bibliophile and a poet.[2]

However, Peter's true passion was history. He collected, read, and had translated the chronicles of several lands. In addition to his chronicle, he had two other historical works written during his reign. The first which he entitled *Compendi Historial* (Historical compendium), is a translation of Vincent de Beauvais's *Speculum Historiale* (Mirror of history). The second, known as both *Crònica general de Pere III, el Ceremoniós* (Chronicle of the kings of Aragon and counts of Barcelona) and *Crònica de sant Joan de la Penya* (Chronicle of San Juan de la Peña), survives in three fourteenth-century manuscripts: Catalan, Latin, and Aragonese.[3]

Peter probably supervised the *Crònica de San Joan de la Penya,* the official record of his reign. It serves as an introduction to Peter's *Chronicle* because it is brief and covers many years of Catalan and Aragonese history, from the legendary and historical accounts of the founders of Iberia to the reign of James II.

Despite sections of literary interest, especially legendary passages, miraculous apparitions, and dialogue, this chronicle lacks the literary merit of the four major Catalan chronicles, due in part to its excessive emphasis of historical detail and to its dry and monotonous style.

Authorship and Date of the *Chronicle*

Scholars generally believed that Peter III wrote his chronicle, until Josep Coroleu published a letter from Peter to Bernat Descoll, approving the material for the first three chapters and for part of chapter 4, and instructing Descoll on the rest of the chronicle.[4] Beginning in 1369 Peter devoted himself during various intervals to the chronicle before his death in 1387.[5] The king directed his chronicle, perhaps by setting forth its outline and by indicating the sources on which to base it.[6] He probably chose additional collaborators: Arnau Torrelles, Ramon de Vilanova, and Bernat Ramon Descavall.[7]

Scholars have also determined that the chronicle was begun before 1349, then continued in 1355 and 1371. The prologue apparently was written between 1367 and 1374.[8] Descoll's letter indicates that the first three chapters were complete in 1375. The remaining chapters were finished by 1383. Peter himself, aided by one or more of his collaborators, revised the work between 1382 and 1385.[9] An appendix, attached to one manuscript and included in the first edition (Barcelona 1527), must have been written later.[10]

Peter considered his *Chronicle* the most important historical work of the three produced during his reign; he had copies made for the archives, for the leading monasteries of his realm, and for the pope (probably a Latin version).

General Characteristics of the *Chronicle*

Peter's *Chronicle* is essentially medieval because of his view of the past, dependence on the supernatural, and insistence on divine providence. However, this work, written when humanistic tendencies began to enter Catalonia, represents an evolution in its genre. It lacks hypothetical prose narratives common to the three major Catalan chronicles, partly because of the decline in the minstrel tradition and partly because of Peter's evolving Renaissance concept vis-à-vis a chivalric interpretation of history, a change that Arthur Terry attributes to modifications in the nature of government: "medieval political structures are reluctantly yielding to a newer and more absolutist conception of monarchy which comes to rely increasingly on the support of the middle classes in its struggle against the aristocracy."[11]

The Purpose of Peter III and His Presence in the *Chronicle*

A reading of the *Chronicle* of Peter III and of studies on the life and letters of this king reveals the political and personal motives underlying this work: (1) Peter wished to assert himself and the monarchy before the nobles and rising mercantile faction; (2) he wanted to reintegrate completely the Catalan confederation and to justify his actions to hold together its political unity; (3) he viewed his work as a manual to instruct his successors; and (4) he desired to ensure his immortality.

Peter's eminent presence makes it impossible to discuss the major themes, motifs, and characteristics of his chronicle without focusing on him. The authors of his *Chronicle* drew his character with precision, insisting that he was capable of passion and error. They also revealed that his inexperience compelled him to take a minor role in government. For example, in chapter 2, Peter admits twice that when he came to power, his youth and inexperience forced him to relinquish arduous decisions to his elder counselors.

Peter appears as a proud monarch, occasionally given to vengeance and cruelty when others threaten the unity of his domain. These severe acts include Peter's punishment of Valencians who promote the Aragonese Union. In one such instance, the barber Gonçalvo, who had insulted and embarrassed Peter and his wife, is humiliated and punished by death in a scene in which Peter becomes sarcastic.[12]

Unlike the protagonists of previous chronicles (James I, Peter II, and James II), Peter III is not an intrepid warrior who enters or engages his forces in battle despite odds against him. Instead, he enters into alliances with the Venetians against the Genovese so that he will receive financial benefits from the union. On two different occasions he admits his reluctance to wage war against the French because the results would be devastating. Furthermore, to avoid confrontation with Henry of Castile, Peter marries his daughter Elinor to his adversary, John I.

In his letter Peter insisted that Descoll admit everything, "even if it be very prejudicial to us."[13] He strove for sincerity, objectivity, and historical realism; however, his chronicle is realistic only in the sense that he limited fantastic accounts and instead based his narration primarily on official documents (*QG*, 121). Peter and his collaborators used fewer legendary episodes than the earlier chroniclers, but those they did use, together with several narratives with epic elements (*C*, 1:85), belie the realism of the chronicle. One legend, the blasphemy of Alphonse the Wise, has political overtones (*C*, 2:493–95). Also, during the battle of Lucisterna, Alphonse the Benign is thrown from his horse in battle, reaches for the magical sword of Vilardell, and kills several soldiers, causing the enemy to retreat (*C*, 1:160).

Following a tendency established in previous Catalan chronicles, Peter reserved his greatest praise for the Catalans, perhaps realizing that the mortar that held together the floundering Catalan-Aragonese empire was Catalonia. Upon entering Catalonia, Peter exclaims: "Oh blessed land, peopled with loyalty! Blessed by Our Lord God who has delivered Us out of a rebellious and wicked country [Castile]!" (*C*, 2:419). Also, Alphonse the Benign alludes to the system called *pactisme* (oaths sworn to by the Catalan king prior to governing each kingdom in his realm, promising that he will respect their laws) when he answers Leonor of Castile's demand for capital punishment: "Queen, queen, Our people are free and are not kept in subjection as are the people of Castile, for they have Us as lord and We them as good vassals and companions" (1:179).

Division, Unity, Style, and Language in the *Chronicle*

Structurally, Peter's chronicle consists of a prologue, six long chapters, and an appendix. The prologue, which discloses a providential idea of history, differs in tone and style from the rest of the chronicle because of its Scholastic structure and biblical references. This style was common to contemporary works, such as the moral-didactic treatises of Francesc Eiximenis.

In the six chapters that form the body of the work, the authors chronologically relate events from Peter's birth in 1319: chapter 1, the succession of James II and the expedition to Sardinia (1319–36); chapter 2, the coronation and first deeds of Peter III as king (1336–40); chapter 3, revolt and war with Mallorca and Roussillon (1341–45); chapter 4, the second invasion of Mallorca and the union of Aragon and Valencia (1345–50); chapter 5, the war with Genoa and expedition to Sardinia (1350–55); and chapter 6, the war with Castile and Peter's dealings with Henry of Castile (1356–75). The appendix or seventh chapter lacks the precise style and chronological order of previous chapters, contains anachronisms and unreliable accounts, and narrates events that followed Peter's death.

The external structure of Peter's *Chronicle* suffers because the prologue and appendix differ in style and tone from the body of the work. The six chapters could be read as separate entities, although occasionally they overlap (for example, the presence of James III of Mallorca and

Leonor of Castile is felt in several chapters). The unity of Peter's chronicle, however, lies in the internal structure derived from the precision and selectivity of each chapter. Unlike Muntaner and, to a lesser extent, Desclot, Peter focused on a single action or major episode and followed it through to its conclusion. Also, the action proceeds in a chronological day-to-day development "per jornades" (C, 2:606), as Peter prescribed to Descoll, and at times resembles a diary. Chapters 2 and 3 are especially significant for their thematic and stylistic unity, dramatic scenes, and personal nature.

In his letter to Descoll, Peter requested repeatedly that his collaborators compose as detailed a chronicle as possible. In their turn, they carried out these instructions and others that Peter prescribed to the advantage and disadvantage of the chronicle. For example, Peter's description of the campaign against Sardinia is far superior to Muntaner's account of the same campaign, due to his selection of material and development of descriptive passages, such as the geography of the island and the action. Peter's concise narration contrasts with Muntaner's exaggerated and amorphous accounts. Besides being selective, Peter and his collaborators used few overly descriptive passages, except for the report of Peter's coronation attire and preoccupation with protocol. However, they often developed personal or circumstantial information: Peter's premature birth; the birth of his daughter; his weeping over the siege of Valencia; his weeping with his faithful followers of Burriana. Also, they included an interesting account of an event that took place in Barcelona preceding the death of Prince James. Peter, upon arriving in this city, called James's attention to a man on a tightrope. The prince admitted he saw nothing and retired to his quarters, where he died a few days later.

At times the authors introduced lengthy explanations to rationalize Peter's political maneuvering, or they composed detailed passages because of their political and social significance. For example, Peter bluntly refused to be crowned king of Aragon by the archbishop of Saragossa—the traditional practice—in order to become politically independent of the church hierarchy (C, 1:196). Also, his indifference to either papal faction during the western Schism made his attitude toward the papacy even more apparent.

The *Chronicle* of Peter III is written in a clear and correct prose, which reflects the spoken language and the prose of the royal chancellery. The influence of the spoken language lends a natural, vivid, and popular quality to the prose, particularly in its frequent dialogues. The direct and precise Catalan idiom of the text is interspersed with other languages:

on one occasion, James III of Mallorca speaks in Provençal; Peter the Cruel, Leonor of Castile, and Castilian nobles speak Spanish with traces of Aragonese, a language spoken by the Aragonese in Peter's train. The authors also reproduce in the final chapters letters written entirely in Spanish with an occasional Aragonese expression. Again, verbal exchanges with Peter speaking Catalan and Castilians replying in Spanish are common.

Scholars attribute the major flaws in style to excessive dependence on documents and historical detail: lengthy lists of participants in treatises or battles; lists of peace proposals, such as the one given to the inhabitants of Collioure; lists of agreements; and reproductions of documents in the final chapters, especially letters sent to Peter by Castilian authorities. Chapter 2, however, appears more spontaneous, especially when compared to chapter 6, because the authors relied less on documentation in the former than in the latter.

Sources and Evaluation in the *Chronicle*

The *Chronicle* of Peter III differs from the other three great Catalan chronicles because it is a premeditated historical work and more documented. Its major sources include oral reports and documents collected and archived by the king's chancellery. For example, for the events transpiring between 1336 and 1351, the authors extensively consulted accounts of the *escrivà de ració,* a subordinate treasury official. They also used the Bible as an indispensable manual. For example, in the prologue they quoted several psalms and parallel their content and significance to the general character of Peter's reign. Biblical references, such as the comparison of the planned destruction of Valencia to Sodom and Gomorrah, continue in the body of the chronicle.

Strong parallels between both works suggest that Peter had read *The Chronicle of James I* mentioned twice in his *Chronicle:* both were written in the first person plural, "nós," and emphasize the astuteness of their protagonists in making decisions. The authors of both works contrasted their protagonists with other peninsular kings. For example, James I and Peter III are resolute while James's Iberian counterparts, Sancho of Navarre and Alphonse X, as well as Peter's contemporaries, Peter the Cruel and James III of Mallorca, are indecisive. The latter two also become cowards who break treatises with Peter and launch attacks on his realm when he is occupied with other matters. Therefore, Peter, who emulated his famous ancestor, used *The Chronicle of James I* as a model and a source of inspiration rather than as a source of factual knowledge.

Conclusion

Despite chronological and factual flaws, the *Chronicle* of Peter III has significant historical and social value. It continues the popular style and realism of the previous three major chronicles, while incorporating changes that reflect a modification in literary taste and the role of government. Despite the complicated process of writing the chronicle (for example, the number of collaborators, the interruptions in elaboration, Peter's diminishing role in supervising the final chapters), its authors avoided repetition and even apologized for repeating one episode that was a necessary preface to a chapter. Peter and his collaborators created personal and spontaneous narratives, especially in the last half of chapter 2 and in chapter 3. They also keep intact Peter's authority and independence throughout.

Many of the flaws in the chronicle can be attributed to the method Peter himself dictated. In his instructions the king emphasized that his collaborators give a day-to-day account. Following his advice, they sacrificed narrative development, gave too much attention to protocol, and included long lists of battle participants, treatise agreements, and verbatim reproductions of letters, all of which stagnate the action. As a result, the chronicle frequently proves tedious reading, a flaw that is especially evident in the description of the Roussillon campaign (1343–44).

Finally, the *Chronicle* of Peter III has exerted little influence outside of Catalonia. After the death of Peter's son Martin I, which marked the end of his dynasty, few Catalans were allowed to read his chronicle, except in the defective Carbonell edition, until the nineteenth century (*C,* 1:82). Subsequently, several Catalan editions have appeared, including one published in France, but to date only a Spanish translation (1850)[14] and the Hillgarths' English translation (1980) have been printed. The severe criticism of Jerónimo Zurita, who doubted the historical precision of the chronicle, may have damaged the credibility of the chronicle and partially diminished its influence.[15]

Chapter Eight

Francesc Eiximenis

Biography

Born in Gerona around 1327, Francesc Eiximenis studied in his formative years with the Franciscans and took their habit. In 1352, according to a document inscribed at the Episcopal Archives of Barcelona, he was ordained deacon at Santa Maria de Sants church in Barcelona. From 1365 to 1370, he traveled through Europe and, like many promising theologians of his time, attended leading universities.

In 1371, supported by the Catalan royal family, Eiximenis went to the University of Toulouse, where he received the Master of Theology degree three years later. He then returned to Barcelona to teach theology and philosophy at the Franciscan convent. As his influence with Catalan dignitaries increased, authorities in Vic and Tarragona sought him for his learning.

Between 1374 and 1382, Eiximenis probably produced several works no longer extant, including four volumes of sermons and several treatises.[1] At this time he began his encyclopedia *El Crestià* (The Christian), a project encouraged by the Catalan king Peter III, who asked that Eiximenis be held in Barcelona until its completion.[2] Eiximenis did in fact finish *Primer del Crestià* (First book of the Christian) in 1380 and started *Segon del Crestià* (Second book of the Christian) before moving to Valencia.

The years in Valencia (1382–1408) mark the height of Eiximenis's literary career. By establishing cordial relations with the *jurats*, the municipal authorities of Valencia, Eiximenis won their support for *Dotzè del Crestià* (Twelfth book of the Christian), his most original work. He received further recognition when the *jurats* promoted and displayed three volumes of *El Crestià* in the City Hall.

Catalan Works: General Characteristics

Eiximenis's most ambitious project, *El Crestià,* was intended as a detailed guide for the faithful. Although he conceived of a thirteen-volume encyclopedia (representing Christ and the twelve apostles), Eiximenis probably did not take his project beyond the four extant books: *Primer* (1379–81), *Segon* (1382–83), *Terç del Crestià* (Third book of the Christian, 1384), and *Dotzè* (1387, 1391). The author had a premeditated plan, audience, and intention for *El Crestià,* which he specified in the *Primer.* He began by discussing religion in *Primer,* proceeded to worldly and human considerations (temptation, sin, evil) in the *Segon* and *Terç,* and intended to end *El Crestià* by discussing celestial rewards in the thirteenth book, which he never wrote. Yet despite this plan, the four extant volumes of his ambitious project differ in subject matter, literary value, and fate. For example, although the *Primer* was printed in 1483, no modern edition of it has appeared. Only two manuscripts exist of *Segon,* which has never been printed. Although readers have been attracted by the social, literary, and political content of *Terç* and *Dotzè,* scholars have published only portions of these two works.

However, when he began writing *El Crestià,* Eiximenis seemed unsure of his audience. For this reason *Primer* and *Segon* lose their direct and personal appeal to a sober Scholastic style. Also, the lack of anecdotes and *exempla* suggests that Eiximenis had not yet developed his personal style of *Terç* and *Dotzè.*

In the first volume of *El Crestià,* Eiximenis identified his audience as laypersons: "First it must be said that in this entire volume, I intend to proceed in a simple and unrefined way, so that although this book can be of profit to learned and well-trained individuals, I intend, rather, to speak to simple laypersons who are not trained in this subject matter."[3] For this audience he simplified and synthesized his theological knowledge, adopted a religious and moral-didactic purpose, and wrote in the Catalan language.

To instruct the layperson Eiximenis created a popular writing style, avoiding abstractions and simplifying his subject by using analogies, tales, fables, contemporary folklore, superstitions, and descriptions of nature, sources common to his contemporary Hispanic prose writers. In the Franciscan tradition he used biblical, patristic, and monastic sources, which he often quoted in Latin and translated, glossed, or paraphrased into Catalan.

Beginning with *Terç,* Eiximenis had developed a sense of audience. For this reason scholars consider *Terç, Dotzè,* and *Llibre de les dones* (Book for women) among his leading literary works due to folk motifs, proverbs, and the balance in popular and erudite styles, and *exempla.*

Furthermore, these treatises represent an excellent source of fourteenth-century Valencian society. Eiximenis meticulously described social practices in eastern Spain, and compared customs (dining, wearing apparel, forms of worship, political and judicial practices) with those of other regions of Spain and of Europe. Because of his descriptions of Catalan and Valencian social practices, Antoni Rubió i Lluch affirmed that Eiximenis recorded late medieval Catalan speculative and political life to the extent that Ramon Muntaner recorded national and historical exploits.[4]

Because of his didacticism, Eiximenis sometimes describes society subjectively, treating it with irony and satire. For example, he ridicules the eating habits of Germans, Italians, and the French, and the new women's fashions brought from France to eastern Spain. In addition, when he wrote *Primer,* he intended to prove that Christianity was the greatest and true religion. He therefore wrote on the religious and social practices of Jews and Moors, revealing popular prejudices and canonical law of the time. He emphasized the Islamic influence on Valencia, a city he described as *quasi morisca* (almost Moorish), in his *Regiment de la cosa pública* (The rule of the state), which he wrote in 1383 as a separate treatise before incorporating it into *Dotzè.*

Writing at a time when socioeconomic changes affected morality and art, and permissiveness and corruption infiltrated education, politics, and religion, Eiximenis popularized Catholic doctrine by using humor, irony, and occasional sarcasm. He arranged this doctrine in chapters according to the scholastic method by providing detailed and, at times, syllogistic argumentation, and divisions and subdivisions to prove his beliefs. He also used two common rhetorical devices: the question and the commentary.[5] For example, he asked a series of questions and then answered each one by giving his opinions on several issues. In the commentary, a more frequent device, he skillfully sustained a discussion of a biblical, classical, or patristic passage for several chapters.

During Eiximenis's time relations between the Catalan-Aragonese empire and other regions of Europe, notably France and Italy, fostered an interest in humanism. However, Eiximenis shunned the humanism and classical style of his contemporaries, translators, and writers of the chancellery, preferring instead the medieval world, which he was attempting to restore. By extolling medieval culture, Eiximenis hoped to revive traditional moral values to guide Christian laypersons toward salvation.

Dotzè contains the most complete nonlegal treatment of the fourteenth-century governmental system of the Catalan-Aragonese empire. Known as *pactisme,* this system consisted of a pact in which the monarch pledged to rule justly and to accept the traditional laws governing each political division of his kingdom. In exchange, the people within the king's territory swore allegiance to him.

To show the advantages of this system, Eiximenis used classical and medieval sources: Aristotle, Valerius Maximus, Pompeius Trogus, Augustine, Gregory the Great, Thomas Aquinas, Boethius, Vegetius. Francisco Elías de Tejada, who describes Eiximenis as the leading medieval Hispanic author of political treatises, regards *Dotzè* as an attempt to reconcile outdated neo-Augustinian ideas with Eiximenis's love for national freedom.[6]

Eiximenis adhered to a theocentric concept of authority, placing ecclesiastical authority above civil government. Therefore, he held the pontiff in greater esteem than his temporal counterpart, the emperor, though both derived their power from God; and he upheld canon law over civil legislation.

Eiximenis divided *Dotzè* into eight parts.[7] Volume 1 contains parts 1–4 (chaps. 1–473), plus additions from 1391 and *Regiment de la cosa pública* (chaps. 357–95). Volume 2 includes the remaining parts and chapters (467–907), subtitled *Regiment de príceps e comunitats* (The Rule of princes and communities).[8]

The material of *Dotzè* is varied but well organized. Eiximenis began this treatise by establishing the need for cities, specifying the qualities, education, and training the prince required, and advising the ruler on how to govern prudently and wisely. He then extended his counsel on good government to include the remaining royal and municipal officials. In short, Eiximenis emphasized in this treatise and others the all-inclusive goal of an orderly Christian society structured on the Pauline analogy of the Mystical Body.

In *Dotzè* Eiximenis continually recommended peace and reconciliation when cities, kingdoms, or rulers were at odds. He also advocated the political philosophy of his native Catalonia, a system of government he espoused and equated with the democratic spirit. The clarity of his theories stems mostly from his ability to analyze and to observe.

Llibre de les dones (ca. 1396), a moral guide to salvation for women, has been divided in two major parts: in chapters 1–13 Eiximenis dealt with women in general and revealed his concept of womanhood; in the remaining chapters, 14–383, he discussed the five states of woman: infancy, maidenhood, marriage, widowhood, and the religious life. From a literary standpoint, the first one hundred chapters (sections 1–4) are the most interesting. Here Eiximenis resorted once more to a popular style, reproducing proverbs, fables, anecdotes, miracles of Mary, picaresque passages on modes of dress, the use of cosmetics, and the risque behavior of women. He also borrowed from popular literature: "the *Book of Fables* reads . . . that the Lord made the tongue of woman from the tail of the goat which wags continually."[9] By using *exempla* and humor, Eiximenis made doctrine more interesting to his audience and satirized unacceptable behavior. In this volume, as in *Terç,* Eiximenis demonstrated a mastery of narrative art, his literary forte. His digressions, refrains, and anecdotes reinforce and personalize his didacticism. As a result, his content, technique, and style make his prose accessible even to the modern reader.

Llibre de les dones, however, is unbalanced: sections 1–4 take up slightly more than one fourth the book while the fifth section (the treatise on the nun) covers chapters 101 to 383. In this fifth section Eiximenis wrote in a more erudite style, thus abandoning the more popular style of his early chapters because of his subject matter—nuns, the religious life, religion, and the ascetic life.

In *Llibre dels àngels* (Book of angels), Eiximenis carefully synthesized the speculative nature of his material (pure spirits), in prose accessible to his nonspecialized audience. He wove into the speculative and scholastic content a vast amount of learning and medieval culture, which he attempted to make concrete in nonclerical terms. He occasionally included interesting references to medieval science and history: the specific remedies of illness (bk. 4, chap. 45); the prophetic-apocalyptic tradition (bk. 5, chaps. 34–43); the visual images which play upon the humors (bk. 4, chap. 57); and the use of spectacles (bk. 4, chap. 38).

By writing this treatise on angels, Eiximenis may have encouraged angel worship in fifteenth- and sixteenth-century Europe for several reasons. After his death *Llibre dels àngels* (1392) became a success as several manuscripts and editions in Catalan, Latin, French, Spanish, and Flemish appeared. In the seventeenth century, Castilian religious and nobles continued to read his treatise on angelology, which influenced the art and literature of Spain and France.[10]

However, modern scholars have neglected *Llibre dels àngels* and have failed to edit books 1–4 for several reasons: the doctrinal nature of the treatises; the lack of social, popular, and folk descriptions, vis-à-vis *Terç* and *Llibre de les dones;* and Eiximenis's overdependence on *Celestial Hierarchy* by the pseudo-Dionysius Areopagite.

In his last years Eiximenis turned to Christology and wrote *Vida de Jesucrist,* also entitled *Vita Christi* (Life of Christ) between 1397 and 1398, modeling it on a medieval tradition established by Ludolph of Saxony's *Vita Christi* and Ubertino de Casale's *Arbor vitae crucifixi Jesu* (The tree of the life of Christ Crucified). Among the major nonbiblical sources of his *Vida de Jesucrist,* Eiximenis included Bonaventure's *Commentaries on the Sentences of Peter Lombard* and the pseudo-Bonaventure's *Meditatione vitae Christi* (Meditations on the life of Christ).[11] Like *Llibre de les dones, Vida de Jesucrist* suffers an imbalance between its parts. The initial chapters on the birth and youth of Christ are the most interesting, for the author bases them on the Apocrypha and medieval traditions (for example, the wounding of Christ by the Egyptian during his exile).

Eiximenis divided his ascetic-mystical work *Scala Dei* (Staircase to God) into three parts: a treatise on the commandments, a discussion of capital sins, and a treatise on contemplation. However, he extended the content of *Scala Dei* beyond the active and contemplative life, by making it a devotional work containing chapters on Christian reconciliation, devotion to Mary and guardian angels, penitence, and the three phases of contemplation. Curt J. Wittlin found that *Scala Dei* was an abridgment of *Llibre de les dones* (sec. 5), an abridgment with three divisions: original prayers, a summary, and a copy of *Llibre de les dones.*[12]

Because *Scala Dei* lacks both the popular appeal of *Terç* and the beginning chapters of *Llibre de les dones,* some scholars classify it among Eiximenis's minor works. Others, however, consider it a serious exposition of Christian devotion and asceticism, a leading treatise on the subject written in medieval Spain, and a possible source for the great mystical tradition of Golden Age Spain. Some even claim that *Scala Dei* directly influenced *Exercitatorio de la vida spiritual* (Exercise on the spiritual life), a work that in turn inspired *Spiritual Exercises* of Ignatius of Loyola.[13]

Conclusion

Francesc Eiximenis became a leading prose writer of Catalonia and a leading moralist and encyclopedist of the late Middle Ages. He wrote during a turbulent era, having witnessed the Black Death, Schism, political upheaval, and social and cultural change. To explain these disasters and changes, he proposed a return to past values, especially to the monastic and Scholastic learning and reforms of the twelfth and thirteenth centuries.

Eiximenis found his greatest inspiration of the Bible, the works of Augustine, Thomas Aquinas, Bonaventura, and other theologians. However, to transmit the ideas of his patristic, monastic, and scholastic predecessors in Catalan to laypersons, he consulted late medieval monastic and sermonic literature. Because of his compulsion to seek authoritative proofs, his works lack originality. Furthermore, this extensive, sometimes excessive, dependence on sources makes his works, like those of Vincent Ferrer, inferior to those of Ramon Llull, who more successfully synthesized and poeticised his sources.

Eiximenis was gifted, however, with a narrative skill that compensates for his ideological conformity. To make theological concepts accessible to laypersons, he used proverbs, refrains, accounts of contemporary customs, anecdotes, and *exempla,* and narrated these in a personal way. To his more popular works, he added humor and irony, thus balancing doctrine and narrative.

Interest in the works of Eiximenis continued in Europe, especially in Spain and France, into the seventeenth century and increased during the epoch of the Catholic kings in Spain and during the Counter-Reformation. His works were translated into Spanish and were read by Spain's royal family and by minor Spanish authors, who fell under his influence.

Few works of Eiximenis have been printed during the last two centuries. A project begun by Spanish Capuchins and Franciscans in the 1920s to edit his works was interrupted by the Civil War.[14] Thereafter, doctoral dissertations of students at the universities of Toronto, Barcelona, and Chicago have elicited renewed interest in Eiximenis; and, more recently, a group of scholars organized in Gerona has begun to publish his unedited manuscripts.[15]

Chapter Nine
Saint Vincent Ferrer

Biography

Born into a middle-class family in Valencia in 1350, Vincent Ferrer became prominent in Western Europe during the late fourteenth and early fifteenth centuries, due primarily to his influence on the Avignon papacy and on the Catalan-Aragonese monarchs. At age seven he received the clerical tonsure and began preparing for the priesthood as a novice in the convent of Saint Dominic near his parents' home. He entered the Dominican order in 1367, and in the ensuing years studied logic in Barcelona, wrote Latin treatises, and accepted a lectureship in logic at the University of Lérida. In 1372 he returned to Barcelona to teach science and philosophy and to study theology. Four years later he was called to Toulouse, where he was ordained in 1378 and where he secured his Master of Theology on the recommendation of Pedro de Luna.[1]

In 1380, a year after his return to Valencia as prior of the Dominican convent in that city, Ferrer completed his defense of the Avignon pontiff, his *De moderno Ecclesiae schismate* (On the modern schism of the church) and dedicated it to Peter III.[2] Because Peter believed that this dedication compromised his neutrality on the papal schism, his cordial relations with Ferrer became strained. As a result, Ferrer renounced the priorship, dedicated himself to preaching, and strengthened his ties with Pedro de Luna. On 9 December 1385, he accepted a professorship at the Cathedral of Valencia, a position he held until 1390, at which time he accompanied Pedro de Luna through Castile and Provence, converting non-Christians and preaching. In 1395 Ferrer went to Avignon as the confessor of Pedro de Luna, who had been elected Pope Benedict XIII the previous year. He served in this capacity until 1398, when illness and a vision changed his life. Convinced that his mission was to preach to all nations and to become a delegate "a latere Christi" (on the side of Christ), he refused a hierarchical position and left the papal court.[3]

During 1399 Ferrer concentrated on converting the infidels and on countering heretical beliefs in France and in northern Europe. After a stay with Benedict XIII in Savoy, he left for northern Italy, where he remained from 1406 to 1407. He spent the following year in Montpellier, before returning to Barcelona.[4]

Saint Vincent played a major role in the Compromise of Capse in 1412. Commissioned by the Valencian authorities to represent them in electing the Catalan-Aragonese monarch, he not only cast the initial vote for the victor, Fernando de Antequera, but was also chosen to announce the council's decision to the populace.[5]

From 1399 to 1409, Saint Vincent developed his sermonic technique and established a pattern that he used until he died. He would arrive where he was invited to preach mounted on an ass and escorted by as many as three hundred followers. This group included Dominicans as well as laypersons and children of different social classes who observed his severe discipline and wore the Dominican habit. Once greeted by the audience, Ferrer would retire to a local friary and prepare the sermons to present the following day after Mass. He addressed the homilies not only to Christians but also to Jews, who were ordered to attend his sermons under the penalty of a fine.[6]

Ferrer left Spain in 1416 and spent the rest of his life in France. He preached in his native Valencian tongue, and yet, according to documents, was understood in France and in other European kingdoms.[7] On 5 April 1419, Saint Vincent died in Vannes and was buried in the cathedral of this city. He was canonized in 1455 by Pope Callistus III.

Sermons: Manuscripts and Editions

In 1927 J. Sanchis Sivera began editing Ferrer's homilies preached during Lent (1413) in Valencia; and in 1932 and 1934 he published a compilation of sermons composed during Saint Vincent's stay in southern France.[8] Recently Gret Schib continued the latter compilation.[9] Aside from these collections, isolated sermons have appeared in journals.

In contrast to the stylistically superior Lenten sermons, some of Ferrer's homilies published by Sanchis Sivera and Schib are more intense and spontaneous. The insipidity of the earlier sermons is due to elaboration by compilers and amanuenses, who synthesized sections and omitted anecdotes repeated from previous works. A recently discovered manuscript indicates that Saint Vincent carefully planned his homilies, although he probably never wrote out a complete sermon in his native language.[10]

Ferrer's sermons were transcribed by *reportadors,* stenographers—usually two—who alternated transcribing his homilies. The stenographers, however, limited themselves simply to taking notes that they later revised. As a result, the written sermons only briefly reflect Ferrer's homilies, which lasted an average of two hours. Joan Fuster, in his extensive study on Saint Vincent's oratory, shows that certain devices, such as the use of "etc." and apparent lapses in the logic of various sentences, indicate the stenographers' omissions and abbreviations.[11]

Structure and Tone of the Sermons

With minor structural deviations, such as the salutation "bona gent" (good people), Vincent Ferrer's sermons conform to the technique Francesc Eiximenis prescribed in his Latin treatise *Ars praedicanti populo* (Art of preaching to the people).[12] These sermons are divided into three sections: the *introductio* (introduction), in which he discusses a biblical passage corresponding to the day's gospel or epistle, salutes the people and recites the *Ave Maria;* the *introductio thematis* (introduction of the subject), in which he repeats the biblical passage, explains it literally, and applies it morally; the *divisio thematis* (division of the subject), a lengthy section in which he explores every possibility of the theme. The sermon often ends with a summary and/or a ritual formula.

Finding his inspiration in the Bible rather than in the classics, Saint Vincent shunned erudite sermons and humanistic tendencies. He directed his vernacular homilies toward the illiterate and the poor, the "poble menut," as he called them. Therefore, unlike Eiximenis, he preferred the spoken word to writing in Catalan.[13] However, like Eiximenis, he wished to remain in a medieval world as his attitude toward classical poets, even Dante suggests:

When a preacher talks about Sacred Scripture and pays no attention to the poets—the Vergils, the Dantes, those meters, etc.—but only to Sacred Scripture, notice that it is not he who preaches, but rather the Holy Spirit or Christ; he is but a bagpipe. Tell me, when the musician plays the bagpipe, tell me, where does the sound come from, the bagpipe or the musician? The musician creates it. Thus, the good moral preacher is the instrument, but Christ is the musician who inflates the will to love, the intelligence to discern, and the memory to recall. (*S,* 2:72)

Ferrer also believed that a homily must be coherent and well-organized: "It is comparable to a net in which one string is joined to another.

Therefore, when the string is pulled in, the entire net follows. The same is true with a well-organized sermon: one example is tied to another, one authority to another; then, when, with one string a man takes in the whole net; in the same way, with one subject a man can join together an entire sermon if it is well organized" (*S,* 2:46). His preoccupation with structure is also reflected in his metaphors and similes on construction and architecture.[14]

Saint Vincent's audience, "you, lay people, who don't know how to read, must eat from the crumbs which fall from the table of sapience" (*S,* 2:29), knew and understood most of the fables, anecdotes, miracles of Mary, and lives of saints he narrated to teach theological beliefs and illustrate moral lessons. The *exempla* in his homilies, beginning with the *semblança* (a short metaphorical passage), have a fixed structure and division in each example: (1) a hypothetical situation; (2) the introduction of a new element to capture the listeners' interest; (3) the question addressed directly to the author; and (4) the moral application of the metaphor:[15]

[1] If a man or woman is within a home burning to the ground and finds an open door to escape, but at the door are three lions, what is the person to do? [2] If he remains, he will burn; if he exits, the lion will get him. [3] How to escape? [4] There is a solution in the beautiful example (Daniel, c. VI). Daniel was in the pit of lions, etc. . . . . Note how the angel descended from heaven and tied the lions. . . . The same is true with each person. If he lives a good life, God will send forth the good angel to chain the devil, for justice and prudence are within him. . . . (*Se,* 3:53)

Exempla in the Sermons

Vincent Ferrer, who modeled his life after that of Christ, used metaphors as Christ used parables. For example, the sun, the moon, a mirror, or an apple illustrated the mysteries, such as the Eucharist, the Immaculate Conception, and the Trinity: "The sun, of its very substance, engenders the ray of sunlight in the same way that a father engenders a son. In the first process, the creation of sunlight, notice that heat is produced; thus that which is exhaled is called the spirit. And, so, you see in the sun, the Trinity" (*S,* 1:123–24).

Saint Vincent also recounted numerous miracles that are more lengthy and developed than the metaphors. He became more conscious of his rhetorical techniques in the hagiographical sermons, which contain his miracles.[16] Ferrer based such miracles on accounts in the *Vitae patrum* (Lives of the fathers) and on oral, traditional, and contemporary miracles (*R,* 8:44–46). His miracles of Mary appear shorter and less stereotyped in theme and structure than those of Eiximenis; in fact, thematically and structurally, they resemble those of Gonzalo de Berceo and Alphonse the Wise. Saint Vincent lyrically developed the following miracle, a variant of Alphonse's Canticle 103:

Let it be known that here was a very devout Benedictine monk, who was a sacristan. And one day after matins and before daybreak he went to church to toll the bell of the early hour and noticed: "Oh, it isn't time yet," for he still had fifteen minutes. "Well, I'll go into the garden." While in the garden he began to concentrate on the tree above, and in doing so, he saw a bird—an angel he thought was a bird—and began to sing. The singing pleased him so, that he became enraptured and spent that day, that month, that year in a trance. And what happened? Four hundred years later he came to and said: "It must be time to toll the bell." He tried to enter the church but could not find the door. "Oh, Mary, where am I?" Finally, he left the garden, wishing to enter the church by another door, and found the monastery totally changed. At last he came upon a monk, who asked him: "Who are you?" "I am the sacristan of this monastery." "And who was your abbot?" "So and so." And it turned out that four hundred years had passed since the former abbot had directed that monastery. (*S,* 1:51–52)

Language, Style, and Oratorical Devices

To convey his basic Scholastic beliefs and his message to the masses, Ferrer modified his homiletic language, style, and content and used examples and other oratorical techniques, such as diminutives, augmentatives, proverbs, and refrains. This reproduction of the language of the people made his homilies important linguistic documents.[17] Apart from biblical and patristic Latin quotations and explanations of Hebrew words (Saint Vincent was proficient in both languages), occasional Spanish terms entered into his sermons, due in part to the number of Aragonese and Castilians in his entourage and his itinerancy throughout northern and central Spain.

Fortunately, the stenographers who transcribed Saint Vincent's vernacular sermons retained literary and oratorical devices such as onomatopoeia to satirize the careless religious practices. "Xa, xa, xa" illustrates the words of a perfunctory prayer; "xam, xam, so s'aram," the disinterested manner in which the clergy read the breviary. Animal noises, such as those of chicks who cry to their father, "Buu! Buu!," remind sinners of their dependence on God the Father (*S*, 1:20). Sinners are cast into hell with a quick "xof," and the burning iron on the skin of Saint Margaret produces a sound "chii, chii" (*R*, 8:57, 9:100).

To a great degree, Ferrer succeeded because he knew his audience and used objects and situations from their environment as moral, liturgical, and sacramental symbols. The confessor and Christ become the physician who cures the individual's illness; heaven becomes a place of dance and happiness, where Christ orders Saint Michael to set out "Chairs, chairs for everyone" (*S*, 1:43); the soul is welcomed into heaven like a guest of honor among relatives: "Oh, Saint Michael, Gabriel, Raphael! Oh, my son Pete, my little Cathy, welcome! Why am I so honored?" "Because the Lord wants it this way" (*S*, 1:49–50). Saint Vincent's mastery of animated dialogue, his expressiveness, and his ability to demythologize the supernatural (for example, by having Christ "snarl his nose" at the sinner attempting to enter paradise), and the use of symbols (sun, moon, mirror), attracted his auditors, especially the common people (*Q*, 1:26–27; *S*, 2:172–74).

In his sermons Saint Vincent also employed gestures and fluctuations in tone. His stenographers, through skillful documentation, supplied a kinesthetic guide to his preaching by means of a few devices: the use of words like "així" (like so), "així alt" (this tall), "així baixa" (this short); and symbols, such as the circle (*S*, 1:235), the sign of the devil, to indicate the haphazard manner in which clerics made the sign of the cross. The stenographers further recorded Ferrer's intense style by lengthening the accented vowel to reflect changes in tone: "Ooi! Ess! Coom!" (How), "Hoomens!" (men), "Doones!" (ladies). And Ferrer sometimes singled out specific auditors, perhaps to get their attention or to point out an evil.[18] In one sermon he lashed out at least twice at a man who was falling asleep at the base of the platform where he was preaching.

Themes of the Sermons

Changes in Europe in the late Middle Ages undoubtedly affected Vincent Ferrer, leading him to envision the impending end of the world. In his oratory he, like Eiximenis, constantly condemned vice. He especially denounced blasphemy, sodomy, innovations in dress and cosmetics, usury, clerical concupiscence, ignorance, and indolence. He also criticized the rich as illustrated in the *exemplum* of the chicken and the falcon (*R*,

7:438). However, he spared the Catalan-Aragonese monarchs, especially Fernando de Antequera, for in several sermons he claimed that the king represented God (*R*, 7:436–37).[19]

Apart from numerous examples from Christ's life that he placed in his homilies, Ferrer contrasted social and moral degeneracy in exemplary hagiographic sermons that he preached on saints' feast days. Some of these homilies, such as the sermons of Saint Paul and Saint Margaret, are among his most belletristic. He included in these homilies the leading Christian traditions, such as Augustine's encounter with the child who wished to place the sea into a small cavity in the sand (*S*, 1:229–30). The tendency toward hagiography not only reflects the Dominican's displeasure with the morality of the times but also points to another medieval commonplace in his homilies—the conviction that Christians of the past led better lives, a belief that foreshadows the apocalyptic trend in his sermons. Unlike leading medieval visionaries, such as Joachim of Flora, who saw in monasticism the only means of countering Antichrist, Saint Vincent proposed biblical knowledge as a major defense (*Q*, 1:162).[20]

Sources of the Sermons

Saint Vincent applied himself assiduously to scriptural studies, carrying the Bible with him everywhere and believing that its content and application were inexhaustible: "If Adam had lived forever and had studied the Bible continuously, he would never have learned the Bible, even if he had lived three million years (*B*, 7:135). By quoting Latin passages from the Bible and not translating them into the vernacular, he gave authority to his catechistic purposes.

True to his oratorical theories, Ferrer drew not only his themes but also most of his *exempla* from the Bible, especially the New Testament.[21] However, in depending excessively on sacred Scripture, he often used biblical examples unconnected with his moral principles. As Joan Fuster notices, he exploited the Bible "in an almost constant violation of biblical text . . . by banalizing and exhausting it in the process of drawing from it a moral lesson."[22] For example, the guitar representing penitence (*S*, 2:232) or the wood of David's guitar (an intentional replacement for the harp) signifying the members of Christ, is inappropriate.

Ferrer also drew amply from the *Lives of the Fathers,* a common monastic source (*R,* 8:46–52). The *exemplum* he created from this collection of hermits' lives is among his best:

A miracle from the *Lives of the Fathers* shows how God lives in each person and how he departs from him because of sin and returns to him through penitence. There once was a hermit who served God, and being tempted went to the city to sell artifacts he had made and to buy bread. On his return he was overcome with temptation and sinned with a woman. And as he sinned he saw a dove issue forth from his mouth. He returned to the hermitage and wept bitterly. The hermit told his fellow monks about the dove, and they prayed for him, heard his confession, and gave him a penance. Having completed his penance, he saw the dove hovering over him high in the sky, descend, and enter his body. (*Q,* 2:115)

But despite Ferrer's dependence on biblical and monastic sources, his Thomistic learning forms the core of his philosophical and theological thought. Scholasticism pervaded the subject matter and the divisions in his sermons. Thus, Saint Vincent brought Thomism to the masses by reducing it to its most simple form. Furthermore, his reverence of Thomas Aquinas, as indicated in the homily preached on this saint's feast day (*Q,* 1:56–63), sets "the reformer of the world" above all other patristic writers, such as Gregory, Augustine, Ambrose, and Jerome, and medieval writers such as Bernard.[23]

Evaluation and Conclusion

Vincent Ferrer brought Christian beliefs and scriptural knowledge to the masses, who rewarded him by acclaiming him one of the most prominent preachers of the time. He catered to the people by reducing Christian morality and theology to their most basic comprehensible level through *exempla,* proverbs, refrains, and other literary and oratorical devices. His sermons stand as linguistic and historical documents of the waning Middle Ages and as examples of the sermonic technique of the period. His logical thinking and his academic learning are apparent throughout the homilies.

The sermons, however, do contain defects: overdependence on biblical sources, weak similes and analogies, continuous repetition of *exempla* and topoi, a lack of variety and originality. Lapses in logical content are undoubtedly due to his stenographers' carelessness. His sermons also suffer from the rigors of the Scholastic method, such as a tendency to divide and overclassify material, rigors which subtract from the imagination, spontaneity, and personal accent in his oratory.

On the other hand, the premeditated structuring of his sermons and their logical development appealed to the intelligence of his followers, particularly the clergy and the more sophisticated members of his cortege. In addition, some sermons, such as those on religious beliefs contained in Volume 3 of his *Sermons,* appear directed to a more educated audience. Unfortunately, these sermons are less interesting, except for the hagiographic homilies, whose narratives have a popular appeal.

The Catalan sermons of Vincent Ferrer have been neglected in the English-speaking world. Few have been translated into English; however, recent presentations by Gret Schib in London and Josep Miquel Sobré in Washington have introduced them to English-speaking scholars.[24] Their work and this chapter will perhaps encourage further study and translation into English.

Chapter Ten
Medieval Catalan Theater

Introduction

Medieval theater in Catalan has received little attention outside of Spain. Until recently, few medieval Catalan plays have been edited, and few modern editions and literary studies have been available to interested scholars.[1] Scholars have also found it difficult to define what comprises this theater and to evaluate it.[2]

Medieval documents, as well as medieval themes and traditions that appear in the sixteenth-century drama, indicate that secular theater existed in medieval Catalonia. Unfortunately, most of this theater has been either destroyed during the centuries or transmitted orally but never recorded. Also, some thirteenth- and fourteenth-century Catalan liturgical plays were either lost or discarded by clerics who revised them in later centuries. On the other hand, monasteries as well as ecclesiastical and municipal libraries preserved manuscripts of Catalan religious plays, some of which exist as fragments of complete plays. As a result, most medieval Catalan plays are anonymous and, in some cases, incomplete, unlike the medieval French plays, which are usually complete works written by known authors (Jean Bodel, Rutebeuf, and Adam de la Halle). As the Middle Ages drew to a close, secular theater began to influence religious plays. Liturgical drama, which had been performed within the churches, was staged in public places or on moving platforms called *roques* or *carros triomfals*. Also, secular characters, such as city dwellers engaged in illegal professions, entered the religious theater.[3]

Religious Drama

Unlike the rest of the peninsula, Catalonia received the Roman-French rite from Charlemagne's time.[4] Because of this ecclesiastical tie, Catalan theater owes its existence and character to the Roman-French rite. Ripoll was closely in touch with French monasteries, such as Saint Martial of Limoges, and from these and other religious and cultural centers, Catalonia became exposed to liturgical plays. After the Roman rite replaced the Mozarabic rite in Castile (1080), liturgical drama reached central Spain via Catalonia.

Pascal Cycle. As early as the ninth and tenth centuries, clerics recited Latin liturgical texts in Catalonia during Holy Week, Easter, and Christmas. Later, they included hagiographical plays in the recitation. As a consequence, Catalan religious drama is classified into Easter (Pascal) and Christmas cycles, Assumption plays (Marian cycle), Old Testament *consuetes,*[5] and hagiographical works.

Catalan liturgical drama of the Pascal cycle developed from Latin liturgical drama, specifically *Visitatio sepulchri* (Visit to the tomb). The *misteris*[6] of the Pascal cycle, which focus on Christ's Passion and Resurrection, date from the thirteenth century and continued in vogue until the eighteenth century. The fourteenth-century Catalan play, *Visitació al sepulcre,* contains language and expressions also reflecting its Provençal influence. The extant fragments—with text in Catalan and stage directions in Latin—indicate a work forceful in tone and simple in language and structure.

Another fourteenth-century work, *Passió* (Passion), survives in the fragmented Didot manuscript (Palma de Mallorca) in an almost complete form. *Passió* features Judas Iscariot's life woven together from three common medieval sources: the Moses story, Oedipus theme, and Apocrypha. Set adrift in a river, the infant Judas is rescued by a servant of the king, who takes him to court. Later Judas kills his father and commits incest with his mother. He becomes an apostle, but when Mary Magdalene pours the ointment on Jesus, he becomes angry, believing that ten percent of its worth belongs to him.[7]

This work is important because it represents an early and original version of the Judas legend in Western Europe. Also, it may have influenced Jacob of Voragine's treatment of the Judas legend contained within the life of "St. Matthias" *(The Golden Legend).*[8]

Presented on Good Friday, *Davallament de la Creu* (Descent from the cross) relates Christ's death and burial procession. Two versions of the play survive: a copy housed at the Cathedral of Mallorca and a fragmented version from Ulldecona (Tarragona). In the Mallorcan manuscript two priests play the Roman soldiers and sing a duet in Latin while they lower Christ's body from the cross. The Ulldecona text, though fragmented, is coherent, sober, and concrete. Its verses, written in the traditional *nova rima* meter (paired octasyllables), contain forceful language, such as the Centurion's monologue, and lyrical and mystical tendencies.[9] Due to its theme and solemnity, *Davallament* escaped ecclesiastical prohibitions in the seventeenth and eighteenth centuries and influenced the Valencian Juan de Timoneda's *Auto de la quinta angustia* (The play of the fifth anguish, 1558), a partial translation of the Catalan work.[10]

Two priests, Pere Pons and Baltasar Sança, wrote *Misteri de la Passió* in 1534, relying on the fourteenth-century *Història de la Passió de nostre Déu Jesucrist* (Story of the passion of our lord Jesus Christ) by two Valencian poets Bernat Fenollar and Pere Martínez. Pons and Sança's rigidity and scholarly tone, plus a mixture of popular and traditional characteristics, suggest that they based this *misteri* on older versions of the work[11] and used a series of short *misteris* to form a unit. The cyclical nature of the *misteris* indicates that they were to be performed at times corresponding to the gospel of Holy Week. In recent years two manuscripts of this play were found at Cervera. As a result the play, which came to be known as *Passió de Cervera* (Passion play of Cervera), was staged and recorded.

Christmas Cycle. The Christmas cycle includes a variety of plays, one representing the Tiburtine Sibyl and the Emperor Octavian, several featuring the birth of Christ and the journey and visit of the Magi, and others depicting pastoral scenes, which include *Pastorets* or Mallorcan *Pastorells*.[12]

The best known and researched work of the Christmas cycle, *Cant de la Sibil.lia* (Song of the Sibyl), is based primarily on the poem of the Erythraean Sibyl. In this work the cleric, richly dressed in semi-Oriental garb, announces Christ's birth and the fifteen signs of Judgment Day. In most Catalan versions the Sibyl, accompanied by two clerics or adolescents, slowly lifts a sword while singing so that, when the chant is over, it is fully raised in the form of a cross.

The origins of this work have been debated.[13] It may have developed from *Processio Prophetarum* (Procession of prophets), contained in a pseudo-Augustine sermon, or from reading chants of the sibylline poem. The prophesy, recited and sung in Latin and Catalan, gradually evolved into an independent work. Today it is still sung on Christmas Eve in the churches of Mallorca and the cathedral of Alguer (Sardinia). Catalan versions of the Sibyl chant also exist today in manuscripts and editions in Barcelona, Urgel, Valencia, and other locations of eastern Spain.

Marian Cycle. The Assumption of Mary is the dominant theme of the Marian cycle. From the early fifteenth century, according to Romeu Figueras, Catalans and Valencians celebrated Mary's ascension date and staged Assumption plays, some of which still exist in manuscripts from monasteries and churches: Santa Maria de l'Estany, Tarragona, Valencia, and Elx (Elche). *Misteri d'Elx,* also known as *Trànsit de nostra Senyora* (The death of our lady), has overshadowed all other Assumption plays in Catalan and, unlike medieval plays, has not undergone obvious modifications in either text or stage directions.[14] Actors present the play each year on 14 August, with a second part on 15 August, singing the text and performing it on two pieces of stage machinery with impressive stage devices.[15] Despite its structural inferiority to other Assumption plays, notably the Valencia and Tarragona *misteris, Misteri d'Elx* became more celebrated, perhaps because of its continuous textual revisions and emphasis on music and staging.

Old Testament *Consuetes.*   The tone and character development of the Old Testament *consuetes* remain simple, reflecting their medieval origin. Furthermore, the *consuetes* may have developed from works of the Pascal cycle, especially from Old Testament prophesies on Christ's death. Their lack of humor, a characteristic of medieval Catalan Pascal and hagiographic plays, also suggests this bond. Chronologically they appeared after the *misteris* of the Pascal and Christmas cycles. As a result, their structure and plot are more complex than the structure and plot of the former works.

Misteri d'Adam i Eva (Misteri of Adam and Eve) presented the creation and fall theme, which became significant in late medieval theater because of its allegorical meaning.[16] Its authors created a unified plot that follows the biblical chronology of creation-fall-flight from Eden. They worked closely with the biblical narration, creating an original dialogue.

The clarity and flexibility of its language and style indicate that clerics reworked *Misteri d'Adam i Eva* in the early sixteenth century. Some of Adam's verses have an obvious moral-didactic intention. For example, in reasoning with Eve over whether or not to eat the forbidden fruit, Adam presents moral judgments. However, Eve's suggestion to eat the fruit turns to insistence and finally wrath (*TB,* 39–40), a rare case of emphasis upon a character's individuality.

The Mallorcan *Consueta del sacrifici d'Isaac* (Consueta of Isaac's sacrifice) is based primarily on legends; in fact, its farewell scene exists only in Jewish legends. Also, Isaac's sacrifice, a prefiguration of the crucifixion, became a popular medieval theme.[17] The exchange between Abraham and Isaac reveals the psychological complexity caused partly by deviations from the biblical text. For example, Abraham, the strong, severe biblical figure, becomes distressed and confused, whereas the submissive Isaac shows moral strength by encouraging the human sacrifice. The dialogue, a strong point, becomes intense especially in the sacrificial scene.

Consueta de Josep (Consueta of Joseph), formerly *Consueta de Jacob,* relates the story of Joseph, including his good fortune in the Pharaoh's court. The sale of the deceived Joseph recalls Christ's sale and betrayal by Judas, a popular medieval theme that forms part of Christ's own passion. The authors modify the biblical account only in insignificant ways, such as altering the number and names of Joseph's brothers and the amount of silver they accept from the merchant.

One of the most complex Old Testament *consuetes,* this play requires added stage machinery, approximately fifty actors, and substantial dramatic action. The play is marred by unclear stage directions and incomplete and ambiguous verses, probably the fault of a careless scribe, weaknesses compounded by the poor condition of the manuscript.

Consueta de Tobies (Consueta of Tobias) taught lessons of confidence in God and of fortitude. Its authors remained faithful to its source, the Book of Tobias, retaining scenes that lack dramatic potential, for example, Tobias's captivity under Sennacherib (*TB,* 66–68). At times, however, they modified their source by supplying vague stage directions and by failing to specify the number of characters.[18]

Representació de Judit (The play of Judith), the longest dramatic work of the Mallorcan book of *consuetes,* has more action (for example, battle scenes) than other Old Testament *consuetes.* Stage directions, hymns, and musical accompaniment make this play one of the most elaborate and extravagant. However, at times, stage directions are cryptic or lacking, omissions complicated because the play takes place in three locations: Bethulia, Holofernes's camp, and Nebuchadnezzar's court. Its verses, written in a uniform meter, often form long discourses, a trait uncommon to other Mallorcan *consuetes.*

Consueta del rei Assuer (Consueta of King Ahasuerus), follows the Book of Esther with few omissions, such as Haman's replacing Esther as the main personage. Actors chant all their dialogued verses to the accustomed hymns that accompany *consuetes.* The text, however, is long, monotonous, and repetitious.

In *Consueta de Susanna,* taken from chapter 13 of the Book of Daniel, Susanna is accused of adultery by two elder judges, a charge that Daniel disproves. When compared to the biblical account, the play reveals some modifications: first, a new character, the emperor Eleazar, appears in the story; second, Susanna's daughters, not her servants, defend her and ask the judge for clemency; third, Samuel and Jacob, who accuse Susanna of adultery, do not represent magistrates. Finally, God speaks to Daniel, rather than through Daniel. Overall, these changes add to the dramatic conflict, humanity, and originality of the play. The text itself, however, poses a difficulty because of its mutilated folios and errors in versification.

Hagiographic Theater.   The hagiographic theater of liturgical origin evolved into *epístoles farcides* (farcical epistles), glossed biblical and liturgical forms, with beginnings in medieval trope singing. Generally written in verse, these plays have little dramatic action, but instead teach a moral lesson. The vernacular appears in these works after the twelfth century.

Based on the Book of Acts, *Epístola farcida de sant Esteve* (Farcical epistle of Saint Steven), written in the thirteenth century, is closely related to the Latin *plantus*. Like most early Catalan works in verse, it bears the imprint of Provençal in its language and form; and even its content may have been based on a thirteenth-century Provençal work. Structurally, it is contained in stanzas of four monorhymed octosyllables.

Epístola farcida de sant Joan (Farcical epistle of Saint John), like the previous work, is a significant document for the linguist, the musicologist, and the liturgist although it has little belletristic value. However, unlike *Epístola farcida de sant Esteve,* the versed hymn on Saint John is shorter, more popular in tone, and influenced by French models rather than by Provençal works.

These two farcical epistles were sung in Latin and Catalan: the Latin verses were sung solemnly, and the Catalan version followed in the form of a hymn, accompanied by music.[19] In this way the faithful who were not schooled in Latin received the biblical message. The plain tone, sobriety, and formulaic expressions in the Catalan text underscore its lack of originality.

Sermó del bisbetó (Boy bishop's sermon), a fourteenth-century religious piece, derives from a popular medieval custom of parodying the holy office.[20] Elected by his peers on the vigil of Saint Nicholas (6 December), the boy bishop served in this feigned capacity during the octave of the Holy Innocents, a custom practiced at Montserrat.

The structure of *Sermó del bisbetó* is simple: in verses 1–25, fellow acolytes present the boy bishop, who delivers his sermon—often composed by an elder—in verses 26–122. Written in *noves rimes,* the monologues are lively, despite the lack of movement in the work, which contains discrepancies in the syllabification and rhyme. The theme of the homily varied, and the tone was often satirical. However, the author of this Catalan rhymed sermon preferred a serious theme, the life of Saint Nicholas. Its simple and expressive language contained formulas common to troubadour verse. Its originality may be due to a hagiographic tradition that began in the religious center from which the sermon proceeds.[21] Tradition informs us that the sermon was occasionally followed by other parodic acts, such as giving the blessing to the congregation or dancing and singing secular songs.

Staged in churches and convents in the late Middle Ages, Catalan hagiographic plays were brief and humorless, and adhered to their sources. Eventually, like some of the old Catalan *misteris,* they became an important part of the Corpus Christi processions.

Hagiographic plays recently published by Romeu Figueras include several with medieval qualities and others with humanistic and Renaissance tendencies. In certain plays, such as *Misteri de sant Eudald* (Misteri of Saint Eudaldo), *Consueta de sants Crispí i Crispinià* (Consuetes of saints Crispin and Crispiniana), and *Consueta de sant Jordi Cavaller* (Consueta of Saint George, the knight), medieval techniques dominate the work: more attention to action than to the main characters; a greater adherence to the source and therefore less originality; detailed stage directions, including the use of stage machinery; *noves rimades* sung to common hymns; more characters; a prologue in which the author asks for silence. On the other hand, two *consuetes (Consueta de sant Mateu, Consueta de sant Francesc)* (Consueta of Saint Matthew, Consueta of Saint Francis) show more modern tendencies: soliloquies and exhortations, pious meditation, absence of singing, division of the play into *passos.* In most hagiographic plays, however, the distinctions are unclear, for authors often combined both medieval and humanistic elements. The *Consueta de la conversió de sant Pau* (Consueta of Saint Paul's conversion) combines action and medieval staging techniques, pious meditation, a moral-didactic purpose, and a more modern verse meter. However, clerics generally wrote plays with humanistic tendencies for cenobites. For example, the *Consueta de sant Francesc* was probably staged during the profession of novices at Palma de Mallorca.

Hagiographic plays have one or more sources, usually *The Golden Legend,* New Testament passages, *Flos sanctorum* or legends common to the Middle Ages. The *Misteri de santa Agata,* although based on *The Golden Legend,* contains secular and Renaissance elements in a precise style and clear language. It was probably copied from an earlier version. The unfinished *Misteri de sant Eudald,* based on legendary accounts of this saint, seems medieval in its form and content and closely resembles Mallorcan *consuetes*. Its bipartite thematic structure, conversion/apostate and passion/death, recurs in many hagiographic plays. Overall, the protagonists of hagiographic plays lack individuality, functioning instead as archetypes or personifications of virtues. The authors subordinate character development to action and spectacle.

The ingenious nature of these plays, however, gives rise to a wealth of symbols and allusions. For example, in *Consueta de sant Jordi Cavaller*, the legend of Saint George (patron of Catalonia) slaying the dragon symbolizes the valor of youth liberating oppressed people. In the *Consueta de la passió de sant Cristofor*, the saint represents fortitude and the triumph of virtue.[22]

The Secular Theater

Although deriving from different origins, early Catalan secular theater developed alongside religious drama. Buffoons, jugglers, and minstrels either interpreted songs and recitations with gestures and mimicry or created rudimentary representations based on dialogued texts. Popular and courtly dances, both of which included dialogue and action, also contributed to the development of secular theater in Catalonia. Also, royal feasts and public celebrations prompted a number of spectacles for entertainment. Such spectacles included *jocs,* military or chivalrous scenes acted out on occasion without dialogue, and *entremesos,* short presentations that included action, song, and dialogue. The latter might contain combat scenes between Christians and Moors, symbolism or allegory acted out in poetry or to music.[23]

The tradition of the *danse macabré* (dance of death) also provided material for the Catalan theater. One of the most famous Catalan texts written on the macabre theme is the Mallorcan *Representació de la Mort* (The play of death), probably written by the poet Francesc d'Olesa i Santmartí, who depended on traditional Catalan verses.[24] Its author wrote the work in five-verse heptasyllables, combining an erudite literary style with colloquial language. But, due to irregularities introduced by errors in the oral tradition and manuscript transmission, some verses are obscure.

During the sixteenth century the theater in Catalan-speaking areas changed. Valencia became a center for the theater, now dominated by the Spanish language, a change reflected in some major works of the period.[25] *La vesita* (The visit), by Joan Fernández de Heredia, and the three farces included in Lluís de Milà's *Cortesano* (The courtier) are Catalan-Spanish bilingual works. These works, along with Fernández de Heredia's *Coloquio de las damas* (Colloquy of the ladies), satirize the bourgeoisie and reflect social interaction between Valencians and Castilians. The works are also a source for the comedy of manners, a popular dramatic form of the Spanish *comedia*.

Several theories explain why Valencian playwrights abandoned Catalan for Spanish: the political unity of Ferdinand and Isabella; the predominant Golden Age theater, featuring authors such as Lope de Vega, Tirso de Molina, and Calderón de la Barca; ecclesiastical prohibitions of religious drama; the failure of Catalan theater to rejuvenate, owing in part to its dependence on religious drama; and the failure to break completely with medieval theater.[26]

The Spanish theater, which engulfed Catalan and Valencian theater, was in turn influenced by this theater. For example, the Passion theme of the Catalan theater affected the religious drama of Golden Age Spain, whereas sixteenth-century Valencian theater had a significant effect on the Spanish theater, especially as a result of Lope de Vega's exile in Valencia beginning in 1588.[27] Therefore, the themes, techniques, and innovations of medieval Catalan drama contributed to and continued in the Golden Age theater of Spain.

Conclusion

Based primarily on religious themes, medieval Catalan theater presented to the faithful biblical texts, the liturgy, and the lives of saints. The plays were traditional, conceived as dramatic sermons providing authors few possibilities for originality. In addition, the moral lesson, spectacle, and ceremony of medieval drama became essential for its creators, who were often less concerned with its literary quality. This traditional and stereotyped character hindered extensive innovations in Catalan theater, contributing to its demise in the sixteenth century. The concurrent formation of European national theaters—the descendants of royal court entertainment—further hastened its decline.

Documents attest that numerous Catalan plays have disappeared. Fortunately, some anonymous fragments still exist, though several, including *Passió de Cervera,* have been revised. Throughout the Middle Ages, clerics and students often reworked religious plays to satisfy changing tastes, to include legends, and to add vitality to traditional works performed annually.

Medievalists who have seen Catalan plays performed in the churches of eastern Spain have been impressed with the stage machinery, spectacle, and solemnity of the stage productions. They contend that much of the quality is lost by casually reading them. Scholars, however, who have located old Catalan dramatic works, prepared new editions, and resurrected documents relating to them, have encouraged further critical and comparative studies. They also believe that these plays should be evaluated as literary works created primarily for moral edification. Through their efforts Catalan drama may one day earn its rightful place among the leading vernacular theaters of medieval Europe.

Chapter Eleven
Conclusions

In the history of medieval Catalan literature, two characteristics stand out: the diverse evolution of poetry and prose and the uniformity of fourteenth- and fifteenth-century erudite prose. Until the fifteenth century, the Provençal language dominated the courtly poetry of Catalonia and, to a lesser extent, popular and religious verse. In addition, Latin models and Provençal literature influenced early Catalan theater. After the coronation of James I (1213), Catalan interest in the politics and culture of Provence declined, because James made Barcelona a political center and then turned his attention to the south, concentrating on conquering Moorish territory. By doing so he unified and extended the Catalan language.

The dearth of Catalan literary manuscripts indicates that Catalan prose developed later than the prose of other Romance literatures. Although texts (fragments of translations and sermonic notes) appear in the twelfth century, not until the mid-thirteenth century do authors use Catalan prose in original works. *The Chronicle of James I*, whose tone resembles that of a rapid conversation, established the style and motifs of later major Catalan chronicles and fifteenth-century prose works.

Ramon Llull transformed Catalan prose into an erudite literary language. To express religious concepts precisely, he often introduced examples from nature but avoided popular expressions and colloquial language. His accurate language, subtle thought, polished prose, and prolixity make him a central literary figure.

In the fourteenth century Catalan prose followed a normal evolution in the major chronicles and religious works. Only Ramon Muntaner strayed from the purity of the language by introducing dialectical expressions and Provençal forms such as the *Sermó*. During this time the unification of the literary language fell to the royal chancellery. Its role in creating a uniform style based on the Catalan of Barcelona explains why few dialectical forms entered the chronicles, Eiximenis's treatises, and translations of legal, scientific, and maritime works. These works reflect the prose style and innovations of scribes at the chancellery.

Because Vincent Ferrer's sermons contain popular expressions, dialectical forms, and diminutives, his homilies provide a linguistic guide to early fifteenth-century Valencian culture. His prose therefore escaped the uniform style imposed by the royal chancellery, especially during the reign of Peter III, who rigorously organized the chancellery. But Ferrer's sermons are not disorganized; on the contrary, his Thomistic training accounts in part for their thematic organization and structural precision.

The Franciscan spirit, with its biblical emphasis, represents a major trait of Catalan religious prose. Llull, Arnau de Vilanova, Eiximenis, Ferrer, and the chroniclers combine the historical and religious character of Franciscanism in their major Catalan prose works. Also, medieval Catalan literature, because of its historical and religious character, tends to be realistic and serious. Occasionally, however, its characteristic sobriety is broken by humorous fables, anecdotes, or *exempla,* which have a moral-didactic purpose. Indeed, didacticism appears throughout medieval Catalan literature and partially explains why the idealistic and fantastic literature written north of the Pyrenees did not take root in early Catalan prose.

Medieval Catalan theater is both religious and secular. Plays that have survived indicate the importance and prevalence of religious drama in Catalan-speaking areas. For example, Catalan literature boasts more Passion plays than any literature except perhaps German. The lack of modern editions and translations have made medieval drama in Catalan relatively unknown outside of eastern Spain. However, recent efforts by Romeu Figueras and others have underscored the value of this theater and added to our knowledge of medieval European theater.

Notes and References

Chapter One

1. Ernest Hoepffner and Prosper Alfaric, *La chanson de sainte Foy* (Paris: Société d'edition Les Belles lettres, 1926), 1:207 2:13.

2. Martí Jampy, "Un poema català del segle XI al Confluent: La *Cançó de Santa Fe*," *La paraula cristiana* 8 (1928):292–307.

3. Martí de Riquer and Antoni Comas, *Història de la literatura catalana*, 4 vols. (Barcelona: Ariel, 1964–66), 1:197–98; on its discovery and sources, see: William D. Elcock, *The Romance Languages* (London: Faber & Faber, 1960), 375–78.

4. The fragment was discovered and published by Anscari Mundó, "Un monument antiquíssim de la llengua catalana," *Serra d'Or*, June 1960, 22–23, and reproduced by Paul Russell-Gebbett, *Mediaeval Catalan Linguistic Texts* (Oxford: Dolphin, 1965), 80. More recently Sebastià Mariner i Bigorra discovered a Catalan document dated 1145; see Carmel Biares, "En la Ribera d'Ebre se escribió el primer documento en catalán," *Correo catalán*, 14 February 1975, 7.

5. Joaquim Miret i Sans, "El més antig text literari escrit en català precedit per una colecció de documents dels segles XI, XII, XIII," *Revista de bibliografia catalana* 4, no. 7 (1904):30–47.

6. William J. Entwistle, *The Spanish Language together with Portuguese, Catalan and Basque* (London: Faber & Faber, 1969), 99.

7. Maurice Molho, "Les *Homélies d'Organyà*," *Bulletin hispanique* 63 (1961):186–210. Joan Corominas pointed out errors in this edition, "Sur les *Homélies d'Organyà*," *Bulletin hispanique* 66 (1964):45–54, before publishing his critical edition: "*Les homilies d'Organyà:* Edició crítica millorada i anotada," in *Entre dos llenguatges* (Barcelona: Curial, 1976), 1:127–53.

8. Elcock, *The Romance Languages*, 439–40; Adnan Gökçen, "The Language of *Homilies de organyà*," in *Catalan Studies in Memory of Josephine de Boer* (Barcelona: Hispam, 1977), 69.

9. Ramon Aramon i Serra, "Augats, seyós qui credets Déu lo Payre," *Hispanic Studies in Honour of I. González Llubera*, ed. Frank Pierce (Oxford: Dolphin, 1959), 1–30.

10. Gregori M. Suñol, "Els cants dels romeus (segle XIV)," *Analecta montserratensia* 1 (1917):178.

Chapter Two

1. Scholars have identified some 250 titles of Llull's works in Latin and Catalan. Unfortunately, all his Arabic works have been lost. For a

91

chronology and classification of his works, see Tomás Carreras Artau and Joaquín Carreras Artau, *Historia de la filosofía española* (Madrid: Real Academia de Ciencias Exactas, Físicas y Naturales, 1939), 1:285–334, and Miguel Cruz Hernández, *El pensamiento de Ramon Llull* (Madrid: Castalia, 1977), 361–403. The *Vita coetanea* was translated into English by E. Allison Peers, *The Life of Ramon Llull* (London: Burns, Oates, & Washbourne, 1927).

2. *Selected Works of Ramon Llull (1232–1316)*, ed. Anthony Bonner (Princeton: Princeton University Press, 1985), 1:10–11; hereafter cited in the text as *SW*.

3. Llull also admitted these visions in an autobiographical poem the *Desconhort* (Comfortlessness, 1295).

4. Ramon Llull, *Obres essencials* (Barcelona: Selecta, 1957), 1:20–21; hereafter cited in the text as *OE*.

5. Miquel Batllori, *Ramon Llull en el món del seu temps* (Barcelona: Dalmau, 1960), 19–21.

6. E. Allison Peers translated this work and titled it *The Tree of Love* (London: Society for Promoting Christian Knowledge, 1926), 14–15. However, most scholars prefer the title *Tree of the Philosophy of Love*.

7. Mark D. Johnson, *The Spiritual Logic of Ramon Llull* (Oxford: Clarendon Press, 1987), 14–15.

8. This classification is not all inclusive, for Llull often combines speculative, social, and didactic elements in individual works. Llull's extensive work, the *Llibre de contemplació en Déu* (Book of contemplation), divided into three long books, contrasts with his short opuscules.

9. Jorge Rubió y Balaguer, "Literatura catalana," *Historia general de las literaturas hispánicas*, ed. Guillermo Díaz-Plaja (Barcelona: Vergara, 1949), 1:689.

10. Modest Prats, "Ramon Llull, 'creador del català literari,' " *L'Avenç* 49 (May 1982):339.

11. Jordi Rubió i Balaguer, *Ramon Llull i el Lul.lisme* (Montserrat: Abadia de Montserrat), 204–11, describes the *Rhetorica nova* as an innovative work that advocates using a simple style.

12. Carreras Artau, *Historia de la filosofía española*, 1:287–88.

13. For a detailed description of its division, see G. Colom Ferrá, "Ramon Llull y los orígenes de la literatura catalana," *Estudios lulianos* 13 (1969):135–37.

14. Rudolf Brummer, "Hi ha un model literari per al *Libre de contemplació en Déu* de Ramon Llull," *Miscel.lània Pere Bohigas. I. Estudis de llengua i literatura catalanes*, (Montserrat: Abadia de Montserrat, 1981), 3:82–86.

15. On the dates of this work (1274–76), see Anthony Bonner, "La situación del *Libre del Gentil* dentro de la enseñanza luliana en Miramar," *Estudios lulianos* 22 (1978):54.

16. Ibid.

17. His presentation, the most natural and interesting of the three, reveals Llull's knowledge of Islam. Armand Llinarès, *Ramon Llull* (Barcelona: Edicions 62, 1968), 197, recognizes Llull himself in this character.

18. For theories on the ending of this work, see Riquer, *Història de la literatura catalana,* 1:244.

19. Bonner, "La situación del *Libre del Gentil,"* 50, 55.

20. Llull held an aristocratic concept of knighthood: merit alone was not sufficient for a man to enter this privileged class he reserved for the nobility.

21. Ramon Llull, *Llibre de l'Orde de Cavalleria,* ed. Marina Gustà (Barcelona: Edicions 62, 1981), 13.

22. Ramon Llull, *Doctrina Pueril,* ed. Gret Schib (Barcelona: Barcino, 1972), 7–8.

23. Ibid., 96–97, 149. The work survived in several manuscripts, in Latin, French, and Spanish translation—sections were translated in Provençal—and in four Catalan editions since the eighteenth century (ibid., 27–35).

24. Riquer, *Història de la literatura catalana,* 1:255–56.

25. Carreras Artau, *Historia de la filosofía española,* 1:610–11.

26. Traditionally, scholars have given the title as *Blanquerna;* however, after finding the form "Blaquerna" in early manuscripts and studying this form, some scholars accept *Blaquerna* as the title Llull intended for this work: see Erhard-Wolfram Platzeck, "El final de *Blaquerna* de Ramon Llull," *Estudis universitaris catalans* 24 (1980):448–50.

27. Ramon Llull, *Blanquerna,* trans. E. Allison Peers (London: Jarrolds, 1925), 29; hereafter cited in the text as *B.*

28. Lola Badia, prologue to *Llibre d'Evast e Blanquerna,* by Ramon Llull, ed. Maria Josepa Gallofré (Barcelona: Edicions 62, 1982), 10.

29. Llull stressed these rhetorical principles in the *Rhetorica nova:* see Rubió i Balaguer, *Ramon Llull i el Lul.lisme,* 211.

30. Lola Badia, introduction to *Libro de amigo y Amado,* by Ramon Llull, trans. Martí de Riquer (Barcelona: Planeta, 1985), xvii–xxii, discusses problems with dating the work.

31. Arthur Terry, *Catalan Literature* (London: Ernest Benn, 1972), 20.

32. Robert Pring-Mill, "Entorn de la unitat del *Llibre d'Amich e Amat,"* *Estudis romànics* 10 (1962–67):49–61.

33. Lola Badia defends the troubadour influence in her introduction to *Libro de amigo y Amado,* xxvii–xxxii. The Islamic thesis is defended by Carlos E. Polit, "Analogías entre el *Libre d'amic e amat* y algunos textos sufíes medievales," in *Actes del I Col.loqui d'Estudis Catalans a Nord-Amèrica* (Montserrat: Abadia de Montserrat, 1979), 171–80; Charles H. Lohr, "Christianus arabicus, cuius nomen Raimundus Lullus," *Freiburger Zeitschrift für Philosophie und Theologie* 31 (1984):57–88.

34. Badia, prologue to *Libre d'Evast e Blanquerna,* 11.

35. Miquel Batllori, *OE*, 1–132, suggests that Llull may have adopted "meravelles" from *mirabilis,* a common term in Latin works of the time, meaning a scientific or spiritual goal. In old French and Provençal the equivalent to "meravelles" meant to marvel, astound, or horrify. Riquer, *Història de la literatura catalana,* 1:302, believes that the name Felix intentionally conveys two concepts: the mythological Phoenix and the Latin *felix.*

36. John Dagenais, "New Considerations on the Date and Composition of Llull's *Libre de bèsties,*" in *Actes del Segon Col.loqui d'Estudis Catalans a Nord-America* (Montserrat: Abadia de Montserrat, 1982), 139.

37. For similarities see *SW,* 2:649–50; see also Joaquim Molas, prologue to *Llibre de meravelles,* by Ramon Llull, ed. Marina Gustà (Barcelona: Edicions 62, 1983), 9–11.

38. On the date of writing, see Dagenais, "New Considerations," 131–35.

39. Llull used the feminine "Na" (Dame) Reynard perhaps because the word "guineu" (fox) in Catalan is also feminine.

40. Rubió i Balaguer, *Ramon Llull i el Lul.lisme,* 319–22, describes this process of selection. See also Edward J. Neugaard, "The Sources of the Folk Tales in Ramon Llull's *Llibre de bèsties,*" *Journal of American Folklore* 84 (1971):333–37.

41. Cruz Hernández, *El pensamiento,* 125–42, provides an excellent introduction and diagrams of Llull's division of this work.

42. For a good study of the *racontaments,* see R. D. F. Pring-Mill, "Els *racontaments* de *L'arbre exemplifical* de Ramon Llull: la transmutació de la ciència en literatura," in *Actes de Tercer Col.loqui Internacional de Llengua i Literatura Catalanes,* ed. R. B. Tate and Alan Yates (Oxford: Dolphin, 1976), 311–23.

43. Rubió i Balaguer, *Ramon Llull i el Lul.lisme,* 289–90.

44. See ibid., 245, for other examples of rhymed prose. The dialogue of the pepper and the rose probably influenced the Nicaraguan poet, Rubén Darío: see Rubió y Balaguer, "Literatura catalana," *Historia general,* 1:697.

45. Carreras Artau, *Historia de la filosofía española,* 1:607–8.

46. *The Tree of Love,* ed. Peers, 35.

47. J. H. Probst, "La mystique de Ramon Llull et l'*Art de contemplació,*" *Beiträge zur Geschichte der Philosophie des Mittelalters* (Münster: W. Aschendorff, 1914), 10.

48. Miquel Dolç, "El sentiment de la natura en l'obra rimada de Ramon Llull," *Estudis romànics* 9 (1961):17–18.

49. Lullism here is understood as the influence of Llull's thought, especially the ideas contained in his works or works attributed to him, from the fourteenth to the eighteenth century.

50. *Anthology of Catalan Lyric Poetry,* ed. Joan Gili (Berkeley: University of California Press, 1953), xxxiii.

51. J. N. Hillgarth, *Ramon Llull and Lullism in Fourteenth-Century France* (Oxford: Clarendon Press, 1971), 159–62.

52. Ibid., 269.

53. Ibid., 274; Paolo Rossi, "The Legacy of Ramon Llull in Sixteenth-Century Thought," *Mediaeval and Renaissance Studies* 5 (1961):188–89.

54. Miquel Batllori, "La fortuna de Ramon Llull a Itàlia," in *Vuit segles de cultura catalana a Europa* (Barcelona: Selecta, 1959), 36.

55. Josep Perarnau, "El diàleg entre religions en el lul.lisme castellà medieval," *Estudios lulianos* 22 (1978):257–59.

56. Frances Yates, "The Art of Llull," *Journal of the Warburg and Courtauld Institutes* 17 (1954):166.

57. Armand Llinarès, "Un aspect de l'antilullisme au XVIIIe siècle: les *Cartas eruditas* de Feijóo," *Bulletin hispanique* 64 (1962):498–506.

58. Riquer, *História de la literatura catalana,* 1:252.

59. A more recent edition was edited by Alfred T. P. Byles (London: Oxford University Press, 1926). For translations, see Ramon Llull, *Livre de l'ordre de chevalerie,* ed. Vincenzo Minervini (Bari: Adriatica, 1972), 21–26.

60. Carlos Clavería, "Sobre la traducción inglesa del *Libro del Orde de Cavalleria* de Ramon Llull," *Analecta sacra tarraconensia* 15 (1942):65–74; W. H. Schofield, *Chivalry in English Literature* (Cambridge, Mass.: Harvard University Press, 1912), 97, 216–18, 285.

61. Helmut Hatzfeld, "The Influence of Ramon Llull and Jan van Ruysboeck on the Language of the Spanish Mystics," *Traditio* 4 (1946):337–74; Helmut Hatzfeld, "El *Llibre d'Amic e Amat* as Forerunner of Classical Spanish Mysticism," *Estudis universitaris catalans* 23 (1979):255–64.

62. Rosalia Guilleumas, *Ramon Llull en l'obra de Jacint Verdaguer* (Barcelona: Barcino, 1955), 65–70, 103–48.

Chapter Three

1. Arnau de Vilanova, *Obres catalanes,* ed. Miquel Batllori, 2 vols. (Barcelona: Barcino, 1947), 1:12; hereafter cited in the text as *OC*. Recently John F. Benton proposed an Aragonese village: "The Birthplace of Arnau de Vilanova: A Case for Villanueva de Jilóca near Daroca," *Viator* 13 (1982):245–54.

2. Manuel de Montoliu, *Ramon Llull i Arnau de Vilanova* (Barcelona: Alpha, 1958), 132.

3. Arnau received little support from Robert of Naples, although he dedicated medical treatises to the monarch, including his *De conservanda juventute* (On the preservation of youth).

4. Majorie Reeves, *The Influence of Prophecy in the Later Middle Ages: A Study of Joachimism* (Oxford: Clarendon Press, 1969), 216, 222–23.

5. José Pou y Martí, *Visionarios, beguinos y fraticelos (Siglos XIII–XV)* (Vic: Editorial Seráfico, 1930), 45–46.

6. Carreras Artau, *Historia de la filosofía española,* 1:207–13.

7. On specific religious beliefs, see Salvador de les Borges, *Arnau de Vilanova, moralista* (Barcelona: Institut d'Estudis Catalans, 1957), 105–13.

8. Francisco Elías de Tejada and Gabriella Pèrcopo. *Historia del pensamiento político catalán* (Sevilla: Montejurra, 1965), 3:59.

9. Arnaldo de Vilanova, *Escritos condenados por la Inquisición* (Madrid: Nacional, 1976), 29.

10. Elías de Tejada, *Historia del pensamiento político catalán,* 3:73–75.

11. José Perarnau, *Dos tratados "espirituales" de Arnau de Vilanova en traducción castellana medieval* (Rome: Iglesia Nacional Española, 1976), 2–3.

12. See George Sarton, *Introduction to the History of Science* (Baltimore: Williams & Wilkins, 1950), 2:893–900.

13. *Brett's History of Psychology,* ed. R. S. Peters (London: Allen & Unwin, 1953), 307.

14. Michael McVaugh, "Arnald de Villanova and Bradwardine's Law," *Isis* 58 (1967):60–64.

15. Carreras Artau, *Historia de la filosofía española,* 1:223.

16. Riquer, *Història de la literatura catalana,* 1:366.

17. Montoliu, *Ramon Llull i Arnau de Vilanova,* 144.

18. Rubió y Balaguer, "Literatura catalana," in *Historia general,* 1:686–87.

19. Marcelino Menéndez y Pelayo, *Historia de los heterodoxos españoles: Obras completas* (Buenos Aires: Espasa-Calpe, 1951), 3:204.

20. Terry, *Catalan Literature,* 24, attributes the logical development and grammatical precision of his prose to his Latin prose studies.

Chapter Four

1. Jaume Massó Torrents, "Historiografia de Catalunya en català durant l'època nacional," *Revue hispanique* 15 (1906): 498–501.

2. Joaquim Molas, *Literatura catalana antiga: Segle XIII* (Barcelona: Barcino, 1961), 39–41.

3. Manuel de Montoliu, "La cançò de gesta de Jaume I," *Butlletí arqueòlogic tarraconense* 1 (1922):177–95, 209–40.

4. Josep de Villarroya proposed a third hypothesis in which he insists that the *Book of Deeds* was written after James's death and based on documents. Because of recent discoveries, this theory is hardly credible: see *Les quatre grans cròniques,* ed. Ferran Soldevila (Barcelona: Selecta, 1971), 35–45; hereafter cited in the text as *QG.*

5. James I, *The Chronicle of James I, King of Aragon,* ed. F. L. Critchlow (Princeton: Princeton University Press, 1934), 1:26; hereafter cited in the text as *CJ.*

6. Lluís Nicolau d'Olwer, "La crònica del Conqueridor i els seus problemes," *Estudis universitaris catalans* 11 (1926):83.

7. Joan Ainaud, "Jaume Sarroca i Jaume I," *Estudis romànics* 10 (1962–67):131–36, believed Sa Roca was the son of James I.

8. Nicolau d'Olwer, "La crònica del Conqueridor i els seus problemes," *Estudis universitaris catalans* 11 (1926):79–83.

9. Ibid., 83–87.

10. E. Martin-Chabot, "Pere Marsili et le *Libre dels feyts del rey en Jacme lo Conqueridor*," *Bibliothèque de l'Ecole de Chartes* 72 (1911):92–99.

11. Montoliu, *Les quatre grans cròniques,* 30.

12. Terry, *Catalan Literature,* 25.

13. Montoliu, *Les quatre grans cròniques,* 23–24.

14. Joan Ruiz i Calonja, *Història de la literatura catalana* (Barcelona: Teide, 1954), 73–74.

15. Manuel de Montoliu, "Sobre la redacció de la *Crònica* d'En Jaume I," *Estudis romànics* 2 (1949–50):27–28.

16. Ibid., 28–55; Ferran Soldevila, *Al marge de la "Crònica de Jaume I"* (Barcelona: Dalmau, 1967), 45–47.

17. Antoni Badia i Margarit, "La 'substitución lingüística' en la *Crònica* o *Libre dels feyts del rey en Jacme,*" in *Philologica hispaniensia in honorem Manuel Alvar* (Madrid: Gredos, 1985), 2:53.

18. Riquer, *Història de la literatura catalana,* 1:416–18.

19. Rubió y Balaguer, "Literatura catalana," in *Historia general,* 1:702.

20. Martí de Riquer, "El mundo cultural en la Corona de Aragón con Jaime I," in *X Congreso de Historia de la Corona de Aragón* (Zaragoza: Institución "Fernando el Católico," 1979), 307.

Chapter Five

1. Bernat Desclot, *Crònica,* ed. M. Coll i Alentorn, (Barcelona: Barcino, 1949), 1:124–74.

2. On surnames in the Middle Ages, see Martí de Riquer, "La personalidad del trovador Cerverí," *Boletín de la Real Academia de Buenas Letras de Barcelona* 23 (1950):91–107.

3. Jordi Rubió i Balaguer, *Consideraciones generales acerca de la historiografía catalana medio-eval y en particular de la "Crònica de Desclot"* (Barcelona: Henrich, 1911), 19.

4. *Chronicle of the Reign of King Pedro III of Aragon,* trans. F. L. Critchlow, 2 vols. (Princeton: Princeton University Press, 1934); hereafter cited in text as *CR*.

5. M. Coll i Alentorn, ed., *Crònica,* 1:117–23.

6. Rubió y Balaguer, "Literatura catalana," in *Historia general,* 1:703.

7. Lluís Nicolau d'Olwer, *Paisatges de la nostra historia* (Barcelona: Llibreria Catalònia, 1929), 129.

8. Ruiz i Calonja, *Història de la literatura catalana*, 77.

9. M. Coll i Alentorn, ed., *Crònica*, 1:15–19.

10. Ferran Soldevila, "Les prosificacions en els primers capítols de la *Crònica de Desclot*," *Boletín de la Real Academia de Buenas Letras de Barcelona* 27 (1958):74–88.

11. Manuel de Montoliu, "Sobre els elements èpics principalment arturians, de la *Crònica de Jaume I*," in *Homenaje ofrecido a Menéndez Pidal* (Madrid: Hernando, 1925), 1:702–7.

12. Josep Miquel Sobré, *L'èpica de la realitat* (Barcelona: Curial, 1978), 104.

13. Riquer, *Literatura catalana medieval* (Barcelona: Diputación y Ayuntamiento de la Ciudad de Barcelona, 1972), 47.

14. Sobré, *L'èpica de la realitat*, 53.

15. M. Coll i Alentorn, ed., *Crònica*, 1:107–14.

16. Ibid., 1:13–105.

17. Michele Amari, *La guerra del Vespro siciliano* (Milan: Hoepi, 1886), 3:228.

Chapter Six

1. The belief that Muntaner spent his boyhood in service to a monastery preparing for the priesthood is doubtful because of the lack of religious references, excluding the Bible, in his chronicle and his attitude toward the clergy: Joan Fuster, introduction to *Crónica* by Ramón Muntaner, ed. J. F. Vidal Jové (Madrid: Alianza, 1970), xix–xxi. References in the text are to the English translation: *The Chronicle of Muntaner,* trans. Lady Goodenough, 2 vols. (London: Hakluyt Society, 1920–1921); hereafter cited as *CM*.

2. The Greek author George Pachymeres wrote a Byzantine view of the conquest: *Histoire des empereurs Michaele et Andronique*, trans. Louis Cousins, 2 vols. (Paris: Damien Foucault, 1685).

3. Sobré, *L'èpica de la realitat*, 78.

4. Written in Provençal verse and modeled on the French epic of Guy de Nanteuil, the "Sermó" illustrates Muntaner's democratic sense, his knowledge of naval warfare, and respect for the principles of troubadour poetry.

5. Riquer, *Història de la literatura catalana*, 1:474.

6. Sobré, *L'èpica de la realitat*, 109.

7. Fuster, introduction to *Crónica*, xxiii.

8. Riquer, *Història de la literatura catalana*, 1:458–59.

9. Fuster, introduction to *Crónica*, xxiii–xxviii.

10. Sobré, *L'èpica de la realitat*, 45–71.

11. Montoliu, *Les quatre grans cròniques*, 105–107; Riquer, *Història de la literatura catalana*, 1:464.

12. *Roman de Jaufré* (Romance of Jaufré) is another source.

13. For information on Muntaner, see the modern Spanish edition edited by Samuel Gili i Gaya (Madrid: Espasa-Calpe, 1954), xxxii–xxxiv. Frances Hernández gave this English title to her translation (El Paso: Texas Western Press, 1975).

14. Ruiz i Calonja, *Història de la literatura catalana,* 88.

15. Eugene Baret, *Espagne et Provence* (1857; reprint, Geneva: Slatkine, 1970), 144.

Chapter Seven

1. Antoni Rubió i Lluch, "La cultura catalana en el regnat de Pere III," *Estudis universitaris catalans* 8 (1914):225–45.

2. Manuel Milá y Fontanals, *De los trovadores de España,* ed. C. Martínez and F. R. Manrique (Barcelona: CSIC, 1966), 443–44.

3. *Crònica general de Pere III el Ceremoniós,* ed. Amadeu-J. Soberanas Lleó (Barcelona: Alpha, 1961), 5–16.

4. Josep Coroleu, "Descubrimiento del verdadero autor de la crónica de Pedro el Ceremonioso," *La España regional* 3 (1887):530–36. Subsequent research revealed that Descoll was probably born in Mallorca and entered Peter's chancellery around 1355 after several years in Sardinia.

5. Eduardo González Hurtebise, "La Crónica General escrita por Pedro IV de Aragón," *Revista de bibliografía catalana* 4 (1904):197–214.

6. Rubió y Balaguer, "Literatura catalana," in *Historia general,* 1:709.

7. Ramon Gubern i Domènech, "Notes sobre la redacción de la *Crònica de Pere el Ceremoniós,"* *Estudis romànics* 2 (1949–50):137–48.

8. Ibid., 140.

9. Ibid., 145; *Chronique catalane de Pierre IV d'Aragon, III de Catalogne, dit le Cérémonieux ou "del Punyalet,"* ed. Amédée Pagès (Toulouse: Edouard Privat, 1941), xliii.

10. Ibid., lvii–lxi, lxv.

11. Terry, *Catalan Literature,* 30.

12. *Pere III of Catalonia: Chronicle,* ed. M. Hillgarth and J. N. Hillgarth (Toronto: Pontifical Institute of Mediaeval Studies, 1980), 2:446; hereafter cited in the text as *C.*

13. Rubió i Lluch, *Documents,* 1:263.

14. *Crónica del rey de Aragón D. Pedro IV el Ceremonioso, o del Punyalet,* ed. Antoni de Bufarull (Barcelona: Alberto Frexas, 1850).

15. Rubió i Lluch, "Estudi sobre la elaboració de la *Crónica de Pere.l Ceremoniós,"* *Anuari de l'Institut d'Estudis Catalans* 3 (1909–10):537–42, 552.

Chapter Eight

1. Martí de Barcelona, "Fra Francesc Eiximenis, O. M. (1340?–1409?). La seva vida—els seus escrits—la seva personalitat literària," *Estudis franciscans* 40 (1928):443.

2. Jaume Massó Torrents, "Les obres de fra Francesc Eximeniç (1340?–1409?)—Essaig d'una bibliografia," *Anuari de l'Institut d'Estudis Catalans* 3 (1909–10):681.

3. *Libre apellat lo primer del Crestià* (València: Llambert Palmart, 1483), fol. 1 (v).

4. *Terç del Crestià*, ed. Martí de Barcelona, 3 vols. (Barcelona: Barcino, 1929–32), 2:10–12.

5. Francesc Eiximenis, *Com usar bé de beure e menjar*, ed. Jorge J. E. Gracia (Barcelona: Curial, 1977), 14.

6. Elías de Tejada, *Historia del pensamiento político catalán*, 3:122–27.

7. Massó Torrents, "Les obres," 606–7.

8. Jill R. Webster, "A Critical Edition of *El Regiment de Príceps* by Francesc Eiximenis" (Ph.D. diss., University of Toronto, 1969), 12–13.

9. *Lo libre de les dones*, ed. Frank Naccarato (Barcelona: Curial, 1981), 1:21.

10. Francesc Eiximenis, *De Sant Miquel Arcàngel*, ed. Curt J. Wittlin (Barcelona: Curial, 1983), 10–12, 29–32.

11. Albert Hauf, "La *Vita Christi* de Francesc Eiximenis, O.F.M. (1340?–1409) como tratado de Cristología para seglares," *Archivum franciscanum historicum* 71 (1978):45–64.

12. Curt J. Wittlin, "Los problemas del *Cerapou* y el *Libre de les dones* de fray Francesc Eiximenis," *Boletín de la Sociedad Castellonense de Cultura* 46 (1970):83–89.

13. Cebrià Baraut, "L'*Exercitatorio de la vida spiritual* de García de Cisneros et le *Tractat de contemplació* de Francesc Eiximenis," *Studia monastica* 2 (1960):234–65.

14. David J. Viera, "La obra de Francesc Eiximenis, O.F.M. (1340?–1409?) en los siglos XV al XVII," *Archivo Ibero–Americano* 39 (1979):23.

15. Lola Badia, "Girona, València i Francesc Eiximenis," in *Homenatge a Joan Fuster* (Gerona: Col.legi Universitari de Girona and Universitat Autònoma de Barcelona, 1984), 95–98.

Chapter Nine

1. José M. de Garganta and Vicente Forcada, *Biografía y escritos de San Vicente Ferrer* (Madrid: Biblioteca de autores cristianos, 1956), 22–23.

2. J. E. Martínez Ferrando and Francina Solsona Climent, "San Vicente Ferrer y la Casa Real de Aragón," *Analecta sacra tarraconensia* 26 (1953):13.

3. Garganta, *Biografía y escritos de San Vicente Ferrer*, 37–38.

4. Elías Tormo, "En el sexto centenario de san Vicente Ferrer," *Boletín de la Real Academia de Historia* 126 (1950):225.

5. Several sermons reflect his concern with Caspe: see R. Chabàs, "Estudio sobre los sermones valencianos de san Vicente Ferrer," *Revista de archivos, bibliotecas y museos* 8 (1903):120–22; Ferrer's sermons, published in volumes 6–9 (1902–3) of this journal are edited by Chabàs, are hereafter cited in the text as *R*.

6. José M. Millas Vallicrosa, "En torno a la predicación judaica de san Vicente Ferrer," *Boletín de la Real Academia de Historia* 142 (1958):189–98.

7. Clovis Brunel, "Un plan de sermon de saint Vincent Ferrier," *Bibliothèque de l'Ecole des Chartes* 85 (1924):115.

8. *Quaresma de sant Vicent Ferrer, predicada a València l'any 1413* (Barcelona: Institució Patxot, 1927); *Sermons*, 2 vols. (Barcelona: Barcino, 1932–34), hereafter cited in the text as *S*. Manuel Sanchis Guarner reedited the 1927 edition: *Sermons de Quaresma*, 2 vols. (Valencia: Albatros, 1973), hereafter cited as *Q*.

9. *Sermons*, 3 vols. (Barcelona: Barcino, 1975–84), hereafter cited in the text as *Se*.

10. Clovis Brunel, "Un plan de sermon de saint Vincent Ferrier," 108–17.

11. *Obres completes* (Barcelona: Edicions 62, 1968), 1:33–34, 37–38.

12. Martí de Barcelona, ed., *Homenatge a Antoni Rubió i Lluch*, 1:301–40.

13. For a comparison of Eiximenis's theories on preaching and Saint Vincent's sermonic structure, see Riquer, *Història de la literatura catalana*, 2:221–25; Juan Beneyto, *El pomo de la espada* (Madrid: Nacional, 1961), 54–58.

14. Francisco Almela y Vives, "Los valores estéticos en San Vicente Ferrer," *Revista de ideas estéticas* 15 (1957):8–11.

15. Vincent Almazan, "L'*exemplum* chez Vincent Ferrier," *Romanische Forschungen* 79 (1967):300–301.

16. Ibid., 306.

17. Fuster, *Obres completes*, 1:126–29; *Quaresma*, 1:30–32.

18. Riquer, *Història de la literatura catalana*, 2:234.

19. Fuster, *Obres completes*, 1:99–100.

20. Josep Torres i Bages, *La tradició catalana* (Barcelona: Balmes, 1935), 2:38–39.

21. Almazan, 310–11, 318–21.

22. Fuster, *Obres completes*, 1:85–86, 89.

23. Ibid., 1:65–66.

24. Gret Schib, "Els sermons de sant Vicent Ferrer," in *Actes del Tercer Col.loqui International de Llengua i Literatura Catalanes*, ed. R. B. Tate and Alan Yates (Oxford: Dolphin, 1976), 325–36; Josep M. Sobré, "Les veus

de sant Vicent Ferrer," in *Actes del Quart Col.loqui d'Estudis Catalans a Nord-Amèrica* (Montserrat: Abadia de Montserrat, 1985), 173–82. Sister Mary Catherine translated a few sermons: *A Christology of Sermons* (London: Black-friars, 1954), pp. 3–211.

Chapter Ten

1. José Romeu Figueras, "La dramaturgia catalana medieval; urgencia de una valoración," *Estudios escénicos* 3 (1958):51–55.

2. Riquer, *Història de la literatura catalana,* 3:493, 495–97.

3. In the *Misteri de santa Agata* (Mystery of Saint Agatha), Afrodísia, a procuress endowed with the Spanish Celestina's cunning, several prostitutes whom she calls her daughters, and a young noble add to the realism of this play.

4. Richard B. Donovan, *The Liturgical Drama in Medieval Spain* (Toronto: Pontifical Institute of Mediaeval Studies, 1958):20–21. Donovan's theory was questioned by Romeu Figueras, "La dramaturgia catalana medieval," 55, and by Solanage Corbin, in *Cahiers de Civilisation Médiévale* 2 (1959):224–26.

5. Romeu Figueras, *Teatre hagiogràfic,* 1:78, took the *consueta* as a sacred dramatic representation which took place in a church or convent to illustrate and increase the understanding of the liturgy. Francesc Curet, *Teatre català* (Barcelona: Aedos, 1967), 28, rejects his interpretation, stating that the *consueta* was the actual book or manuscript that contains the dramatic work. Ferran Huerta Viñas, *Teatre Bíblic: Antic Testament* (Barcelona: Barcino, 1967), 24 (hereafter cited in the text as *TB*), specifies that the word originally meant a church and cathedral book used to record habitual ceremonies, but in the sixteenth century *consueta* took on the alternate meaning that Romeu Figueras also ascribed to it: the dramatic representation. In this more recent sense, *consuetes* include biblical, hagiographic, allegorical, and other religious plays.

6. The word *misteri* should be understood as a short religious and didactic play, usually staged at Christmas, Holy Week, or Easter. The term was also extended to include biblical and hagiographic plays.

7. Joseph Romeu Figueras, "La Légende de Judas Iscarioth dans le Théâtre Catalan et Provençal," in *Actes et Mémoires du Premier Congrés International de Langue et Littérature du Midi de la France* (Avignon: Palais du Roure, 1957), 82.

8. Ibid., 81, 83.

9. Josep Romeu Figueras, "Els textos dramàtics sobre el *Davallament de la Creu* a Catalunya, i el fragment inèdit d'Ulldecona," *Estudis romànics* 11 (1962–67):118–22.

10. Ibid., 112–13.

11. Jordi Carbonell, "*La Passió*. Misteri dramàtic del segle XVI. (Tinell, Barcelona)," *Serra d'Or* 4 (1962):45–46.

12. Josep Massot i Muntaner, "Notes sobre la supervivència del teatre català antic," *Estudis romànics* 11 (1962–67):56–71.

13. Ibid., 80–87, for bibliography, manuscripts, and text. See also Donovan, *Liturgical Drama*, 165–67.

14. Josep Romeu Figueras, "El teatre assumpcioniste de tècnica medieval als països catalans," *Estudis universitaris catalans* 26 (1984):262–64; Jesús-Francesc Massip, *Teatre religiós medieval als països catalans* (Barcelona: Edicions 62, 1984), 148–78.

15. The *mangrana*, a gilded cloud which, when opened, revealed an actor representing an angel singing in a precarious position. The *araceli*, an aerial platform that is twice lowered and raised carrying actors who sing and play instruments, and on which the image of Mary is placed. A smaller artifice is superimposed on the *araceli*; on it appear the three actors who represent the Trinity and receive Mary.

16. The play consists of 278 verses of *codolada*, a common meter in Catalan poetry made up of an unspecified series of alternating long and short verses with parallel rhyme.

17. Similarities include obedience and submission to the father, fortitude of the sacrificed, the sacrificial lamb of God, ascent carrying wood for the sacrifice, and preoccupation of the mother who fears her son's death. Of the Old Testament plays, the *Misteri de Adam i Eva* appears in a manuscript at the Municipal Archives of Valencia. The remaining six plays in this section are found in the Llabres Codex (manuscript 1139 of the Library of Catalonia).

18. These include: *Alme laudes, Rabi, Christe qui lux, Passio*. Other hymns common to *consuetes* are *Martir Dei, Plant, Verbum supernum, Pange lingua, Rex eterne, Veni Creator, In exitu Israel, Vexilla regis, Anant, anant.*

19. Romeu Figueras, *Teatre hagiogràfic*, 1:16–20.

20. Ibid., 1:30.

21. Ibid., 1:31.

22. Jordi Carbonell, "Sobre teatre medieval," *Serra d'Or* 2 (1960):22. Some hagiographic works are in fact divided into two separate *consuetes*, such as the *Consueta de sant Cristòfor* (Consueta of St. Christopher) and *Consueta de la passió de sant Cristòfor* (St. Christopher's Passion).

23. The popularity of *entremesos* in fifteenth-century Valencia was documented by Jordi Rubió i Balaguer, *La cultura catalana del Renaixement a la Decadència* (Barcelona: Edicions 62, 1964), 143–46.

24. A recent edition of his work has appeared in Josep Massot i Muntaner's *Teatre medieval i del Renaixement* (Barcelona: Edicions 62, 1983), 99–137.

25. On the other hand, Bartolomé de Torres Naharro's *Seraphina* is written in Catalan.

26. Rubió i Balaguer, *La cultura catalana del Renaixement a la Decadència*, 151–52; "La dramaturgia catalana medieval," 75–76; Jaume Fuster, *Breu història del teatre català* (Barcelona: Bruguera, 1967), 14–15.

27. For a leading study on the topic, see Rinaldo Froldi, *Lope de Vega y la formación de la comedia* (Salamanca: Anaya, 1973), 39–90.

Selected Bibliography

PRIMARY SOURCES

1. Catalan Works
a. *Cançó de Santa Fe*
La chanson de sainte Foy. 2 vols. Paris: Société d'edition Les Belles letres, 1926.

b. *Forum judicum*
Mundó, Anscari. "Un monument antiquíssim de la llengua catalana." *Serra d'Or* 2 (June 1960):22–23.

c. *Homilies d'Organyà*
Coromines, Joan. *Entre dos llenguatges.* 2 vols. Barcelona: Curial, 1976, 1:127–53.

d. Ramon Llull
Doctrina Pueril. Barcelona: Barcino, 1972.
Libre de Evast e Blanquerna. 4 vols. Barcelona: Barcino, 1935–54.
Llibre de meravelles. 4 vols. Barcelona: Barcino, 1931–34.
Obres essencials. 2 vols. Barcelona: Selecta, 1957–60.

e. Arnau de Vilanova
Obres catalanes. 2 vols. Barcelona: Barcino, 1947.

f. Four Major Chronicles
Les quatre grans cròniques. Barcelona: Selecta, 1971.

g. James I
Libre dels feyts. 9 vols. Barcelona: Barcino, 1926–62.

h. Bernat Desclot
Crònica. 5 vols. Barcelona: Barcino, 1949–51.

i. Ramon Muntaner
Chrònica. 2 vols. Barcelona: Barcino, 1927–52.

j. Peter III
Cronica general de Pere III el Ceremoniós. Barcelona: Alpha, 1961.
Chronique catalane de Pierre IV d'Aragon, III de Catalogne, dit le Cérémonieux ou "del Punyalet." Toulouse: Edouard Privat, 1941.

k. Francesc Eiximenis
Com usar bé de beure e menjar. Barcelona: Curial, 1977.
Contes i faules. Barcelona: Barcino, 1925.
De Sant Miguel Arcàngel. Barcelona: Curial, 1983.
Lo libre de les dones. 2 vols. Barcelona: Curial, 1981.
Regiment de la cosa pública. Barcelona: Barcino, 1927.
Terç del Crestià. 3 vols. Barcelona: Barcino, 1927–32.

l. Vincent Ferrer
Sermons. 5 vols. Barcelona: Barcino, 1932–84.
Sermons de Quaresma. 2 vols. Valencia: Albatros, 1973.

m. Medieval Catalan Theater
Teatre bíblic: Antic Testament. Barcelona: Barcino, 1976.
Teatre hagiogràfic. 3 vols. Barcelona: Barcino, 1957.
Teatre profà. 2 vols. Barcelona: Barcino, 1962.

2. English Translations
a. Ramon Llull
The Art of Contemplation. New York: Macmillan, 1925.
Blanquerna. London: Jarrolds, 1925.
The Book of Beasts. London: Burns, Oates & Washbourne, 1927.
The Book of the Lover and the Beloved. New York: Macmillan, 1923.
Selected Works of Ramon Llull. 2 vols. Princeton: Princeton University Press, 1985. Besides a translation of several works by Llull, Bonner's study contains a succinct and comprehensive biography and bibliography of Llull's works, including manuscripts and translations.
The Tree of Love. London: Society for Promoting Christian Knowledge, 1926.

b. Chronicles
The Chronicle of James I, King of Aragon, Surnamed the Conquerer. 2 vols. London: Chapman & Hall, 1883.
Chronicle of Muntaner. 2 vols. London: Hakluyt Society, 1920–21.
Chronicle of the Reign of King Pedro III of Aragon. 2 vols. Princeton: Princeton University Press, 1934.
Pere III of Catalonia: Chronicle. 2 vols. Toronto: Pontifical Institute of Mediaeval Studies, 1980.

SECONDARY SOURCES

1. Bibliographies

Badia i Margarit, Antoni M.; Massot i Muntaner, Josep; and Molas, Joaquim. "Situación actual de los estudios de lengua y literatura catalanas." *Norte* 11 (1970):5–160. Pages 67–84, compiled by Massot i Muntaner, provide a good evaluation of medieval Catalan works and criticism for 1950–69.

Brummer, Rudolf. *Bibliographia Lulliana: Ramon-Llull-Schrifttum 1370–1973.* Hildesheim: H. A. Gerstenberg, 1976. The most comprehensive unannotated bibliography on Llull to date.

Diccionari de la literatura catalana. Edited by Joaquim Molas and Josep Massot i Muntaner. Barcelona: Edicions 62, 1979. A useful reference work.

Massó Torrents, Jaume. "Les obres de fra Francesch Eximeniç (1340–1409?). Essaig d'una bibliografia." *Anuari de l'Institut d'Estudis Catalans* 3 (1909–10):588–692.

Ruiz i Calonja, Joan, and Roca i Pons, Josep. "Medieval Catalan Literature." *The Medieval Literature of Western Europe.* Edited by John H. Fischer. New York: Modern Language Association of America, 1966. Although the reference work is in need of revision, the compilation and annotations are useful.

Viera, David J. *Bibliografia anotada de la vida i obra de Francesc Eiximenis.* Barcelona: Dalmau, 1980. This bibliography to the year 1978 is being revised to include a much needed index.

2. Histories of Catalan Literature

Molas, Joaquim. *Literatura catalan antiga.* Barcelona: Barcino, 1961. Volume 1 of a three-part series that contains a brief analysis and a good selected bibliography.

Riquer, Martí de, and Comas, Antoni. *Història de la literatura catalana.* 4 vols. Barcelona: Ariel, 1964–66. The most complete and authoritative work of its kind. Volumes 1–3 deal with medieval literature.

—————. *Literatura catalana medieval.* Barcelona: Ayuntamiento de Barcelona, 1972. A condensed Spanish version of the above work.

Roca-Pons, Josep. *Introduction to Catalan Literature.* Bloomington: Indiana University, Department of Spanish and Portuguese, 1977.

Romeu, Josep. *Literatura catalan medieval.* Barcelona: Barcino, 1961. Volume 2 of a series (see Molas's book with this title). Its sections on religious prose and drama are useful.

Rubió y Balaguer, Jorge. "Literatura catalana." In *Historia general de las literaturas hispánicas,* edited by Guillermo Díaz-Plaja, 1:643–765. 6 vols. Barcelona: Vergara, 1949–67.

Ruiz i Calonja, Joan. *Història de la literatura catalana.* Barcelona: Teide, 1954.

Terry, Arthur. *Catalan Literature.* London: Ernest Benn, 1971. Succinct and penetrating analysis.

3. Books and Articles on Special Topics
a. Early Works

Mediaeval Catalan Linguistic Texts. Edited by Paul Russell-Gebbett. Oxford: Dolphin, 1965. Especially valuable for its examples of tenth- to thirteenth-century Latin and Catalan texts.

b. Ramon Llull

Carreras Artau, Tomás, and Carreras Artau, Joaquín. *Historia de la filosofía española.* 2 vols. Madrid: Real Academia de Ciencias Exactas, Físicas y Naturales, 1939. A solid study on Llull's philosophy and the chronology of his works, which has been updated in recent studies.

Cruz Hernández, Miguel. *El pensamiento de Ramon Llull.* Madrid: Castalia, 1977. Presents the Arabic influence on Llull's thought.

Johnson, Mark D. *The Spiritual Logic of Ramon Llull.* Oxford: Clarendon Press, 1987. A good, up-to-date study on Llull's logic and his Art.

Peers, E. Allison. *Ramon Llull: A Biography.* London: Society for Promoting Christian Culture, 1929.

Pring-Mill, Robert. *El microcosmos lul.lià.* Palma de Mallorca: Moll, 1961. Indispensable study for the understanding of Llull's Art.

Rubió i Balaguer, Jordi. *Ramon Llull i el lul.lisme.* Montserrat: Abadia de Montserrat, 1985. A collection of studies on Llull by a leading authority on medieval Catalan literature along with an informative introduction by Lola Badia.

Sansone, Giuseppe E. "Ramon Llull narratore." In *Studi di filologia catalana.* Bari: Adriatica, 1973. Pages 184–204 provide insights into Llull's prose and his vision of reality.

Urvoy, Dominique. *Penser l'Islam: les présupposés islamiques de l'Art de Lull.* Paris: J. Vrin, 1980. Excellent study on Llull and Islam.

c. Arnau de Vilanova

Paniagua, Juan A. "Vida de Arnau de Vilanova," *Archivo iberoamericano de historia de la medicina y de antropología médica,* 3 (1951), 3–83. A valuable study on the life and medical works of Arnau.

Pou y Martí, José M. *Visionarios, beguinos y fraticelos catalanes.* Vic: Seráfico, 1930. Pages 34–100 contain a comprehensive study on Arnau's heterodoxy.

Santi, Francesco. "Orientamenti bibliografici per lo studio di Arnau de Vilanova, Spirituale," *Arxiu de textos catalans antics,* 2 (1983), 371–95. Comprehensive study on research published between 1968 and 1982.

d. Four Major Chronicles

Montoliu, Manuel de. *Les quatre grans cròniques.* Barcelona: Alpha, 1959. Authoritative summary study of the four major chronicles by one of the most knowledgeable scholars in this field.

e. *The Chronicle of James I*

Nicolau d'Olwer, Lluís. "La *Crònica* del Conqueridor i els seus problemes," *Estudis universitaris catalans,* 11 (1926), 79–88. Informative and succinct on the problems of authorship and manuscript tradition.

f. The *Chronicle* of Bernat Desclot

Sobré, Josep Miquel. *L'èpica de la realitat.* Barcelona: Curial, 1978. This recent study is an especially good analysis of Muntaner's style and gives insights into Desclot's chronicle.

g. *The Chronicle of Ramon Muntaner*

Muntaner, Ramón. *Crónica.* Ed. and Transl. J. F. Vidal Jové. Madrid: Alianza, 1970. The introduction by Joan Fuster to this Spanish translation, despite lapses in organization, contains revealing insights and a solid analysis.

h. *The Chronicle of Peter III*

Gubern i Domènech, Ramon. "Notes sobre la redacció de la *Crònica de Pere el Cerimoniós.*" *Estudis romànics,* 2 (1949–1950), 135–48. Well-documented study on the authorship of Peter's chronicle.

Rubió i Lluch, Antoni. "Estudi sobre la elaboració de la *Crònica de Pere.l Ceremoniós,*" *Anuari de l'Institut d'Estudis Catalans,* 3 (1909–1910), 519–70. Despite the early date on which this study appeared, it remains one of the most comprehensive works of Peter's chronicle.

i. Francesc Eiximenis

Bohigas, Pere. "Idees de Fra Francesc Eiximenis sobre la cultura antiga," *Estudis franciscans,* 42 (1930), 80–85. A good study on the medieval character of Eiximenis's works.

Hauf, Albert G. "La *Vita Christi* de Fr. Francesc Eiximenis (1340?–1409) como tratado de Cristología para seglares," *Archivum franciscanum historicum,* 71 (1978), 37–64. An informative study on the *Vita Christi* and the Franciscan influence in Eiximenis's thought.

Ivars, Andrés. "El escritor Fr. Francisco Eximénez en Valencia (1383–1408)," *Archivo Ibero-Americano,* 14 (1920):76–104; 15 (1921):289–331; 19 (1923):359–98; 20 (1923):210–48; 24 (1925):325–82; 25 (1926):5–84, 289–333. An indispensable study on Eiximenis's activities in Valencia, which contains a valuable historic and thematic study of several works.

Martí de Barcelona. "Fra Francesc Eiximenis, O.M. (1340?–1409?). La seva vida—els seus escrits—la seva personalitat literària," *Estudis franciscans,* 40 (1928):437–500. Informative and comprehensive study.

Wittlin, Curt J. "Los problemas del *Cercapou* y el *Libre de les Dones* de Fray Francesc Eiximenis." *Boletín de la Sociedad Castellonense de Cultura* 46 (1970):61–95.

j. Vincent Ferrier

Fages, P. H. *Histoire de Saint Vincent Ferrier.* 2 vols. Paris: Maison de la bonne presse, 1893–94. Despite its date, this biography is still considered the most reliable study on Ferrer's life.

Fuster, Joan. "L'oratòria de sant Vicent Ferrer." In *Obres completes.* Barcelona: Edicions 62, 1968. Volume 1 (23–151) contains a basic and comprehensive study into most literary characteristics of Ferrer's sermons.

Martínez Ferrando, J. E., and Solsona Climent, Francina. "San Vicente Ferrer y la casa real de Aragon." *Analecta sacra tarraconensia* 26 (1953):1–143. Well-documented and trustworthy biographical study.

Rico, Francisco. *Predicación y literatura en la España medieval.* Cadiz: Universidad Nacional de Educación a Distancia, 1977. A good chronological study of the sermons in medieval Spain and the importance of Vincent Ferrer in its development.

k. Medieval Catalan Theater

Donovan, Richard B. *The Liturgical Drama in Medieval Spain.* Toronto: Pontifical Institute of Mediaeval Studies, 1958. A basic study of the medieval Hispanic theater.

Massip, Jesús-Francesc. *Teatre religiós medieval als països catalans.* Barcelona: Edicions 62, 1984. Focuses primarily on Assumption plays and provides valuable insights into religious theater, especially the importance of religious theater as a spectacle.

Massot i Muntaner, Josep. "Notes sobre la supervivència del teatre català antic." *Estudis romànics* 11 (1962):49–101. Especially reliable study on religious and popular theater in Mallorca.

Romeu Figueras, Josep. "La dramaturgia catalana medieval. Urgencia de una valoración." *Estudios escénicos* 3 (1958):51–76. A good summary study of medieval Catalan theater.

————. "El teatre assumpcionista de tècnica medieval als Països Catalans." *Estudis universitaris catalans* 26 (1984):239–78. Comprehensive and succinct work on the medieval Assumption plays in Catalan-speaking areas by a leading authority on medieval Catalan drama.

Index

Acher *La Corónica* 17, 2 spring 88

Patricia J. Boehne, *Journal of Hispanic Philology* 13 (1988)

· Philip D Rasico *Catalan Review* III, 1 (89)